GREAT
BRITISH CARS
of the 1920s – 1970s

GREAT
BRITISH CARS
of the 1920s – 1970s

Bounty
Books

This edition published in 2015 by Bounty Books,
a division of Octopus Publishing Group Ltd
Carmelite House
50 Victoria Embankment
London, EC4Y 0DZ
www.octopusbooks.co.uk

An Hachette UK Company
www.hachette.co.uk

Publisher Samantha Warrington
Art Director Miranda Snow
Managing Editor Karen Rigden
Project editor Mariangela Palazzi-Williams
Designer www.ummagummacreative.co.uk
Picture Researcher Sophie Delpech
Senior Production Controller Peter Hunt
Written by Fid Backhouse, Kieran Fogarty and Sal Oliver

First published in 2009 by Bounty Books, a division of Octopus Publishing Group Ltd

ISBN: 978 0 7537 3012 6

A CIP catalogue record for this book is available from the British Library

Printed and bound in China

10 9 8 7 6 5 4 3 2 1

Publisher's note
This book is intended to give general information only. The publisher, author and distributor expressly disclaim all liability
to any person arising directly or indirectly from the use of, or any errors or omissions in, the information in this book.
The adoption and application of the information in this book is at the reader's discretion and is their sole responsibility.

Contents

Introduction

Within these pages, you'll find cars of all sorts, shapes and sizes – from tiny microcars to gigantic behemoths, from stately sedans to death-defying racers, produced in Great Britain from the 1920s through to the 1970s.

It is extraordinary to think that just over one hundred years ago Queen Victoria's long reign was drawing to a close, at the end of an era that saw the dramatic unfolding of a world-changing Industrial Revolution in Western Europe and the beginnings of serious industrialization in the USA, a superpower in waiting. History doesn't record what the elderly Queen thought of those new-fangled horseless carriages that started appearing on Britain's streets – but in 1896 the law that required road-going 'locomotives' to be led by a pedestrian carrying a red flag was repealed, allowing 'light locomotives' to proceed at a dizzying 14 mph (22 km/h). 'The Century of the Automobile' had dawned.

In due course, the building of cars would become the world's single most important manufacturing sector, both in its own right and – more significantly – by generating massive spin-off economic growth. Nowhere was this truer than in the USA. That vast young country acquired its first coast-to-coast motor route, the Lincoln Highway, in 1913 and the way in which economic activity and prosperity spread along its entire length like wildfire was a blueprint for things to come, as the automobile rapidly opened up a continent. Meanwhile, oil production to fuel those burgeoning internal combustion engines became a boom industry. In those early years car manufacture attracted a host of clever engineers, eager entrepreneurs and downright chancers who started operating in almost every country of the developed world. The decade before World War I saw rapid technological advance, and by the dawn of the Roaring Twenties, foundations for the modern automobile had been well and truly laid.

This book tells the fascinating story of the motorcar's extraordinary evolution in Great Britain from the 1920s to the 1970s, by highlighting some of the most iconic vehicles ever produced in this country. These are the ones that we'd all love to drive if we were lucky enough to get the chance, for they encompass the most important, interesting, exciting or desirable cars ever built here – often with all four qualities represented in one car. The reason that the car is deeply entrenched in the affections of so many – and remains an unflagging object of desire – is that it represents the ultimate expression of personal freedom. Once that basic motivation is established, the car is capable of stirring all sorts of other emotions, especially if it is a vintage model. Cars can be beautiful works of automotive art or thrilling driving machines, status symbols or vital workhorses . . . even a serious investment proposition. It is no accident that many of the cars featured in these pages come with hefty price tags, as competition to own these very special classics from the annals of British motoring history drives prices to dizzy heights.

Of course, globally the automobile's huge success has created problems. With the people of emerging nations keen to share motoring freedoms long enjoyed in the industrialized world – China is now challenging the USA as the largest single automobile market – the problem of vehicle emissions contributing to the rapid advance of global warming can only become more severe. At the same time, the very things that make the car so desirable in the first place – fast, convenient and flexible personal transport coupled with the freedom of the open road – are slowly being smothered by the sheer volume of traffic. Realistically, there's no way that drivers will be persuaded to give up cars en masse, nor any possibility that people around the world will abandon their dreams of joining the empowered motoring fraternity.

Hopefully, in future, we might be able to drive safer, more efficient, less polluting but still beautiful cars. Maybe that state-of-the-art vehicle will be even developed and produced in Britain. For now though, whether your fantasy is to roar off behind the wheel of a Jaguar E-Type – 'the most beautiful car ever made', according to Enzo Ferrari –be swept off in a chauffeur driven Rolls Royce Silver Cloud II, take to the motorway at top speed aboard an Aston Martin Vantage V8, go for a Sunday drive down country lanes in a Morris Minor or even just spend your days tinkering with your old MG, Great British Cars of the 1920s-1970s is a book to linger over, dream with and thoroughly enjoy.

1920s & 1930s

Alvis Speed 25

FIRST MANUFACTURED:
1936 (until 1940)
ENGINE:
3,571 cc OHV Straight Six
PERFORMANCE:
Top speed of around 90 mph
(145 km/h)
YOU SHOULD KNOW:
The end of the line for the Speed 25 came in late 1940, production ceasing abruptly when the Luftwaffe bombed the Alvis factory in Coventry – and when the company resumed car manufacture in 1946 it was with the solid but much-less-glamorous TA-14.

One car every dashing man about town coveted in the 1930s was the gorgeous Alvis Speed 25 – a sleek machine that would never fail to look super-stylish arriving outside a stately home ahead of that discreetly decadent country-house weekend. Opinions haven't changed. Many classic car aficionados consider the beautifully proportioned Speed 25 to be one of the finest vehicles produced in the 1930s – not only for its stunning appearance, but also for advanced technical features that characterized all Alvis cars and make them a pleasure to drive today.

The marque produced its first vehicles in 1920 and continued in business until the 1960s. Although Alvis built various saloons, the company's real forte was the sports tourer. The powerful Speed 25's immediate predecessor, the racy Speed 20 series, was introduced by Alvis after a brief foray into front-wheel drive with the pretty, innovative but not-very-successful 4/15s and 8/15s of the late 1920s.

This splendidly stylish Alvis sports Saloon is an enduring 1930s' design classic.

Capitalizing on their sporty reputation, Alvis produced the popular Silver Eagle in 1928 with the option of a two-seater, coupe, drophead coupe or saloon body. The Speed 20 Series followed in 1932, ushering in the spectacular flowering that Alvis enjoyed in the 1930s. This came to a climax with the introduction of the Speed 25 in 1936, and who can say how far the company would have developed this superb model if World War II had not intervened.

Three types of Speed 25 were manufactured – a two-door sports tourer, a two-door drophead coupe and a two-door sports saloon. Today, these sought-after classics command top prices, and their quality build has ensured that over half the production run has survived. Anyone lucky enough to slip behind the wheel of a Speed 25 (over 200 are out there somewhere) will be effortlessly transported back to the Golden Era of Alvis.

Austin 7

FIRST MANUFACTURED:
1922 (until 1939)
ENGINE:
747 cc Straight Four
PERFORMANCE:
Most models had a top speed of
50 mph (80 km/h)
YOU SHOULD KNOW:
The Austin 7 name had such
resonance that the company recycled
it twice after World War II – firstly on
A30 models of the early 1950s and
then on the mould-breaking Mini in
1959.

If there's one quintessential British pre-war car it must surely be the Austin 7, one of the most popular small cars ever produced. After a slow start in 1922 with barely two thousand 'Sevens' sold, progress was spectacular. Before the outbreak of World War II abruptly ended production in 1939, over 290,000 had rolled off the line in Britain. Overseas manufacture was licensed in France, Germany and the USA, whilst Japan's reputation for copying others' technology was partially established when Nissan used the Austin 7 as the template for its first cars.

This iconic 'people's car' owed its inception to Sir Herbert Austin, who bulldozed his board of directors into sanctioning a 'big saloon in miniature' and personally designed it in conjunction with Stanley Edge, who was responsible for the engine. The first production model was the AB Tourer. With a wheelbase of just 6 ft 3 in (1.9 m) and weighing in at a mere 794 lb (360 kg) it used a small, economical engine mounted on an A-frame chassis. This may be one of the easiest 'must-drive' cars to find, but double-declutching should be mastered before taking to the road.

There were six types produced over time – tourers, saloons, cabriolets, sports, coupes and vans – most with many variants as technical advances were regularly introduced. In addition, the distinctive two-tone Austin 7 Swallow was coachbuilt by William Lyons of the Swallow Sidecar Company. A Swallow open tourer was introduced in 1927 with a saloon following in 1928. Some 3,500 Swallows were produced in various body styles before Lyons started making his own SS (later Jaguar) cars in 1932. He backed a good pony. By the end of the 1920s the runaway success of the Austin 7 had effectively wiped out most other small British cars and cyclecars.

*The dinky little 'people's car'
came in many shapes and sizes.*

Bentley 8L

It was the last of the line – and the most impressive. The 8 litre Bentley made its debut at the Olympia Motor Show in 1930 and caused a sensation. It was the largest car hitherto made in Britain and a serious competitor for the Rolls-Royce Phantom II. This was W O Bentley's shot at producing a headline-stealer that would catapult him to the top of the luxury car league, thus stealing Rolls-Royce's mantle and rescuing Bentley from financial difficulty.

The ploy was a gallant failure. Only one hundred 8Ls were produced and by mid-1931 Bentley Motors was bankrupt. W O Bentley thought the receiver's sale would see Napiers of Acton emerge with the assets and was already planning a Napier-Bentley with his new partner. But Rolls-Royce, slyly acting through an intermediary, outbid Napier and promptly killed off the 8L.

It was a clever move. The 8L posed a formidable challenge to anything Rolls-Royce made. A state-of-the-art engine offered innovatory features like twin-spark ignition and four valves per cylinder, plus a sturdy chassis with servo-assisted brakes all round, making this an exclusive but expensive vehicle. Bentley Motors supplied a rolling chassis (in short or long wheelbase) and the customer was required to employ a coachbuilder to add bodywork.

Famous names like H J Mulliner, Gurney Nutting and Barker duly obliged, creating a variety of body styles. Most were built on the long chassis, with relatively few buyers choosing the short version. Although the idea was to compete with the luxury saloons of the era, around 20 8Ls were finished with stunning open-topped bodies and even the limousines tended to have racy lines. Whatever bodywork was chosen, the package offered incomparable smoothness and quietness of ride and these magnificent machines are a pleasure to drive, now as then.

FIRST MANUFACTURED:
1930 (until 1931)
ENGINE:
7,983 cc Straight Six
PERFORMANCE:
Over 100 mph (161 km/h) with the heaviest limousine coachwork.
YOU SHOULD KNOW:
With their exemplary build quality, many of the Bentley 8Ls that were manufactured are still around, but such is their cachet that well-restored examples sell at auction for up to $1.5 million . . . and beyond.

The Bentley was sold in chassis form with the purchaser's choice of body added by an independent coachbuilder.

Lagonda V12

FIRST MANUFACTURED:
1938 (until 1939)
ENGINE:
4,480 cc V12
PERFORMANCE:
Top speed around 105 mph
(170 km/h)
YOU SHOULD KNOW:
These supreme machines are very exclusive, and still reserved for the wealthiest of drivers today – fewer than 200 Lagonda V12s were hand-built and they top many a classic-car wish list.

When his company went bust in the early 1930s, W O Bentley soon bounced back, joining Lagonda to head the tech team after the company was rescued from bankruptcy in 1935. Ringing in his ears were the words of new Lagonda boss Alan P Good: 'We have to produce the best car in the world and have only two years'. This demanding task was achieved and, if the Lagonda V12 wasn't the world's finest, it was certainly one of the most interesting cars produced in the 1930s.

Bentley's team designed an innovative V12 power plant that delivered more horsepower than any comparable non-supercharged engine. The chassis was also special, with an advanced suspension

It's not hard to work out that the Lagonda V12 was designed by the former Bentley team.

system that delivered an ultra-smooth ride, always a major consideration with wealthy clients. Equally important was the fact that the chassis was available in three sizes – short, medium and long.

This enabled a discerning customer to choose any body style, with the long chassis perfect for grand limousine bodies and the shortest for speedy roadsters. Fabulous shapes were created in-house by Frank Feeley, reflecting the decline of independent coachbuilders, though some striking bodies were still constructed outside. Varieties included limousines, saloons, tourers, coupes and dropheads.

Two of the most attractive V12s were a pair hastily prepared to compete in the 1939 Le Mans 24 race. They performed brilliantly, finishing third and fourth overall with 'The Old Number Five' winning its class. Another lightweight version beat the lap record at the famous Brooklands circuit – setting a mark of 120 mph (190 km/h), ironically beating a Bentley in the process. Sadly, the outbreak of World War II saw an end to the brilliant Lagonda V12, which would otherwise have become an all-time great if W O Bentley had been able to continue its development.

MG TA

FIRST MANUFACTURED:
1936 (until 1938)
ENGINE:
1,292 cc OHV Straight Four
PERFORMANCE:
Top speed of 79 mph (127 km/h)
YOU SHOULD KNOW:
Although the vast majority of the 3,000
or so MG TAs that were produced
came with factory bodies, some
very attractive customized TAs were
constructed by top coachbuilders like
Park Ward.

Morris Garages were the car dealers in Oxford who customized existing cars, then began producing their own vehicles in the mid-1920s. This led to the establishment of the MG company in 1928 after successive moves to larger premises, culminating in the takeover of an old leather factory at Abingdon where MG remained until production controversially ceased in 1980.

Early output consisted of basic body-on-frame sportcars like the Speed Model Tourer, L2 Magna, NA Magnette Tourer and MG PB, though two-seater racers were also produced. This established an evolutionary line leading to the MG T series that made its first appearance in 1936 with the TA Midget, after MG merged with the Nuffield organization. This typically British open-top two-seater enjoyed considerable success in its own right and pointed the way to a post-war generation of sports cars that would include more MGs, Austin Healeys and Triumphs.

MG's existing chassis design was used but updated to take a Morris 10 engine that was tuned and teamed with twin SU carburettors to give the sort of nippy performance MG enthusiasts expected. But the introduction of hydraulic brakes and a synchromesh gearbox didn't please all MG addicts, despite making the TA easier to drive than its rough-and-tumble predecessors and opening up a wider general market for MG sportcars. Initially, two-seater open and closed versions were offered, the latter rejoicing in the name of 'Airline Coupe'. But this was soon replaced by the Tickford Coupe with its three-position folding soft top.

The MG TA Midget was replaced by the TB in 1939, the latter looking very similar but having a smaller, more modern engine, again borrowed from the Morris 10. But World War II spoiled the party and few TBs (only 379) were produced, though the post-war TC of 1945 hardly differed.

Everyone agrees that the pre-war MGs paved the way for a series of great British sports cars.

Rolls-Royce Silver Ghost

Ford wasn't the only company that clung to a model that served the company well, and – whilst it couldn't be further away on the automotive spectrum – the signature Rolls-Royce Silver Ghost was contemporaneous with Ford's famous Model T. There was a slight difference in numbers, with over 15 million Model Ts sold as opposed to just 7,874 Silver Ghosts, but each defined its own market section and set a benchmark for others to chase.

As the Roaring Twenties got under way, the Silver Ghost was still the car of choice for most really wealthy buyers on both sides of the Atlantic, having been around for 15 years and established an enviable reputation for quality build, absolute reliability and a comfortable ride in the process. In fact, Rolls-Royce prosaically described this enduring icon as the 40/50 hp (horse power) series, and only one car initially had the name 'Silver Ghost' – which press and public soon attached to the whole series.

This was an aluminium-painted 40/50 with silver-plated fittings and open-top body by Barker that took part in the Scottish reliability trials of 1907 and then – packed with journalists – set endurance record after endurance record in the course of a punishing 15,000 mile (24,000 km) test over Britain's rough roads. Don't expect to drive that one – it's owned by Bentley Motors and insured for $35 million.

Reputation made, the series duly dominated the embryonic luxury car market, finally being officially named 'Silver Ghost' in 1925. In pioneering times when cars were unreliable, the Rolls-Royce 40/50 stood out as the exception to the rule. Its robust engine and sturdy chassis ensured enduring success, with no more than periodic technical updates. Its appearance never dated – buyers were able to select custom-built contemporary bodies in the style of their choice.

FIRST MANUFACTURED:
1907 (until 1926)
ENGINE:
7,036 cc or 7,428 cc Straight Six
PERFORMANCE:
Late models with lightweight bodies reached 85 mph (137 km/h)
YOU SHOULD KNOW:
To take full advantage of the world's most important car-buying market, over 1,700 Silver Ghosts were produced at the Rolls-Royce company's American factory in Springfield, Massachusetts between 1921 and 1926.

Rolls-Royce Phantom III

FIRST MANUFACTURED:
1936 (until 1939)
ENGINE:
7,338 cc OHV V12
PERFORMANCE:
Typical limousine-bodied cars could
do around 90 mph (163 km/h) and go
from 0-60 mph (97 km/h) in 17 secs
YOU SHOULD KNOW:
Despite introducing the Phantom III's
highly successful V12 in 1936, it would
be 1998 before Rolls-Royce returned to
this engine format with the delectable
Silver Seraph.

After cheerfully sticking with the Silver Ghost for nearly two decades, Rolls-Royce started introducing new models on a regular basis in the 1920s and 1930s, splitting the enlarged range into two lines – standard and premium cars. The Phantom series was emphatically the latter, reaching a peak of luxurious development with the Phantom III. The Phantom series was introduced to replace the venerable Silver Ghost in 1925, the Phantom I being a handsome straight six built both in Britain and America and the Phantom II following in 1929, featuring a much improved chassis.

In 1936, the Phantom III saw the introduction of Rolls-Royce's first V12 engine, an aluminium beauty with an unusual twin-spark ignition system that gave the car exceptional acceleration and a silky-smooth ride. This advanced machine had in-built jacking, a chassis lubrication system operated by internal lever, independent front suspension and servo-assisted brakes. It was unveiled at the

1935 Olympia Motor Show and lauded as the world's most technically advanced vehicle . . . a reputation maintained to this day with some experts boldly claiming that Henry Royce's swansong design was the best car ever made (he died in 1933).

The compact engine was arranged in a more forward position than on previous Phantoms, allowing greater space for an attractive range of custom bodywork. Some of the better-known Phantom III body styles include the Park Ward limousine, Mulliner saloon and Hooper sedanca de ville. But the ones that are really coveted today are the fabulous drophead coupes by the likes of James Young, for that ultimate 1930s' wind-in-your-hair luxury motoring experience. Just 727 Phantom IIIs were built, but such was their quality that most are still rolling. Production ended when World War II broke out, and when car manufacture resumed in 1947 it was with the Silver Wraith.

The pleasing Phantom III was Henry Royce's last design and proved to be an enduring classic.

The stylish Wraith could cruise all day as it transported those lucky enough to own one.

Rolls-Royce Wraith

The Wraith was designed to be at the heart of the Rolls-Royce standard range, being introduced in 1938 as successor to the 20/25 of 1929 and 25/30 of 1936. It was built at the company's Derby factory and supplied to independent outside coachbuilders as a rolling chassis only, allowing them to design and build whatever body style might be specified by the customer.

As the smooth straight-six engine was designed for high-speed cruising, most body types were saloons with sharp art deco lines, notably the Park Ward limousine and saloon, but also the H J Mulliner four-light touring saloon and Hooper limousine. Other famous firms that produced distinctive bodies such as the occasional cabriolet, sedanca de ville (town car) or flowing roadster included Windover, Thrupp & Maberly and Youngs of Bromley.

Although it was a junior sibling of the Phantom III, the Wraith shared many of the latter's technical features, including the independent front suspension that made it superior to its predecessor, the 25/30 model. Build quality was as always excellent, ensuring that Rolls-Royce maintained its prestige despite offering a cheaper model, and the success of more affordable cars like the Wraith allowed the top-of-the-range Phantom to be offered at a very competitive price.

Around 490 Wraiths were produced before World War II put an abrupt end to production, but the highly regarded Wraith name lived on in a completely revamped model that was the first Roller to reappear after the war, this time with the added prefix 'Silver'. Because of the short production run, pre-war Wraiths are very rare and extremely desirable, as practically every example has classic late '30s lines that delight the eye and most survivors drive as well today as they did on the day they were made.

FIRST MANUFACTURED:
1938 (until 1939)
ENGINE:
4,257 cc Straight Six
PERFORMANCE:
Top speed of 85 mph (137 km/h)
YOU SHOULD KNOW:
Field Marshal Bernard Montgomery was never one to hide his light under a bushel, and the great wartime commander liked to be seen out and about around Deep Cut army camp in his Wraith (vanity registration number FLD 99), which had a rare touring limousine body by Park Ward.

SS Jaguar 100

After cutting his engineering teeth on motorcycle sidecars and customized Austin Sevens, William Lyons moved on to his true life's work – the design and manufacture of Jaguar cars. But first the Swallow Sidecar company built a few SS cars, registering the SS Cars name in 1934. By combining beautiful styling with affordable prices, the company rode the Depression well. SS cars were available as coupes, tourers and saloons and the 1935 SS Mk II looked uncannily like a post-war MG.

In 1935 came the SS90 sportscar, so called because it boasted a top speed of 90 mph (140 km/h), but this pioneering model only lasted one year (with only 23 manufactured) before it was replaced by the SS Jaguar 100, the first to use this iconic name. One of the most attractive cars ever sculpted, this long, low flying machine was impressive to drive and stunning to look at. Two engine sizes were offered – the 2.5 litre and 3.5 litre – and as the name boldly suggested these streamlined beauties could top the magical 'ton' with the windscreen folded flat. Most SS Jaguar 100s were factory-bodied roadsters, but a single coupe was made and a few chassis were supplied to external coachbuilders.

SS continued to produce a bread-and-butter line of saloon cars, and after the pause in production caused by World War II the company returned as a maker of saloon cars, but the SS Jaguar 100 was not revived and Jaguar would not resume production of sports cars until the splendid XK120 appeared in 1948 to adopt the mantle of its fabled cousin. Collectors of classic cars adore the SS Jaguar 100, but few get the opportunity to drive one – only 198 2.5 litre models and 116 of the 3.5 litre version were made, ranking these amongst the rarest and most desirable of pre-war sportcars.

FIRST MANUFACTURED:
1935 (until 1940)
ENGINE:
2,563 cc or 3,485 cc OHV Straight Six
PERFORMANCE:
Top speed of 101 mph (163 km/h);
0-60 mph (97 km/h) in under 11 secs
YOU SHOULD KNOW:
Although the SS 100 bore the model name Jaguar, it was only in 1945 that SS Cars officially became Jaguar Cars as the company was renamed after its popular pre-war model – a move dictated by the negative connotation of 'SS', which had become indelibly associated with Nazi horror.

One of the most attractive cars ever sculpted, the SS Jaguar 100 was also the first model to use that iconic name.

1940s

Allard J2/J2X

FIRST MANUFACTURED:
1949 (until 1954)
ENGINE:
Assorted American Ford V8s
3.6 l (220 cid) to 5.4 l (331 cid)
PERFORMANCE:
Top speed varied according to the
engine, but was typically around
120 mph (193 km/h); 0-60 mph
(97km/h) in 7.4 secs.
YOU SHOULD KNOW:
One American driver who raced
an Allard was Carroll Shelby, who
subsequently used the formula of light
British sports car body teamed with
beefy American engine to create the
iconic AC Cobra.

These custom-built flyers were the brainchild of South London car trader Sydney Allard, who produced an extraordinary assortment of innovative vehicles, manufacturing around 1,900 cars between 1936 and 1954. Of those, fewer than 180 were the Allard company's most sensational machines – the brilliant J2 (90 built) and J2X (83 built) competition roadsters. These were the final fruit of Allard's pre-war experiences building one-off cars for customers who wished to compete in trials events. Sydney Allard found that American V8 engines with massive torque were ideal for the rugged terrain encountered when trialling, setting a pattern for his post-war racing cars, the J2 and J2X.

The J2 was but one model launched by Allard after World War II (he also introduced the J, K, L, M and N road cars) – but proved to be the headliner. The American sports car market was wide open, and Allard's advanced J2 chassis with independent suspension (available as the J2X with a special enclosed Le Mans body) was designed to take a succession of powerful American V8 engines, creating a high power-to-weight ratio that generated sensational performance. This not only made J2s potent competition cars, but also endeared them to American racers whose mechanics could work with familiar home-grown power plants rather than exotic European imports.

Success duly followed on both sides of the Atlantic, with many race wins recorded. A commendable third place in the 1950 Le Mans 24 was followed by a win in the 1952 Monte Carlo Rally, with Sydney Allard driving. But other manufacturers with more resources copied his cars and by the mid-1950s Allard's presence as a manufacturer effectively ended. Find one of the surviving J2/J2Xs if you can, because the effort will be worthwhile – driving one of these awesome machines just once in a lifetime should be every classic-car racer's dream.

The Allard's American V8 engine helped to make this British car a great success in the USA, where fancy European engines were regarded with suspicion.

Armstrong Siddeley Hurricane

The Armstrong Siddeley Hurricane was patriotically named after the famous World War II fighter aircraft.

After a succession of mergers, the Hawker Siddeley group emerged as the producer of Armstrong Siddeley cars – and when World War II ended one of the first models announced was the slinky two-door, four-seater Hurricane drophead coupe. The name shamelessly appealed to patriotic feelings generated by the exploits of the group's wartime Hurricane fighter planes (a companion saloon car was named after the Lancaster bomber).

So the stylish 2 litre Hurricane 16 appeared in 1945, with the Hurricane 18 following in 1949 – a similar model but fitted with a larger engine. The related Typhoon sports saloon (named after another Hawker fighter plane) was essentially a Hurricane with fixed hard top. The reason Armstrong Siddeley was the first British manufacturer able to resume post-war car production was that the company promised to put the emphasis on exports – and indeed the first two Hurricanes built were sent to America, where they completed an impressive coast-to-coast drive from New York to Los Angeles to generate favourable publicity.

One interesting feature of the Hurricane was the optional Wilson gearbox. This allowed gears to be preselected with a hand lever, and subsequently engaged with a 'change' pedal that replaced a conventional clutch. This made for smooth, fast gear changes and versions of this innovative system were used on buses, military vehicles and racing cars produced by other companies.

Just over 2,600 Hurricanes were built, but despite generally robust build quality only a few hundred survive – the chassis did tend to rust where it passed under the rear axle and the Hurricane had yet to acquire classic status when the Ministry of Transport (MOT) roadworthiness test was introduced in 1960. Sadly, as time passed plenty of Hurricanes went to the scrapyard – along with many other fine cars that their owners wish they still had today.

FIRST MANUFACTURED:
1945 (until 1953)
ENGINE:
1,991 cc or 2,309 cc Straight Six
PERFORMANCE:
Top speed of 70 mph (120 km/h);
0-60 mph (97 km/h) in 29.7 secs
(Hurricane 16)
YOU SHOULD KNOW:
Those driving Hurricanes on today's roads often use cars with retro-fitted overdrive gearboxes, as the low-geared originals are not ideal for high-speed cruising on dual carriageways and motorways.

Out of the original production of over 2600 Hurricanes, only a few hundreds survive today.

OTE 985

Austin A90 Atlantic

FIRST MANUFACTURED:
1948 (until 1952)
ENGINE:
2,660 cc Straight Four
PERFORMANCE:
A top speed of 92 mph (148 km/h) was claimed, with a 0-60 mph (97 km/h) time of 16.6 secs
YOU SHOULD KNOW:
The A90 was not replaced when it was discontinued, but the engine lived on in the classic Austin Healey 100 sports car and another Austin A90 appeared in 1954 – though this was the entirely different Westminster model.

Oops! The launch of the Austin A90 Atlantic at the 1948 Earls Court Motor Show in London was a gallant but misguided attempt to create a post-war export winner by appealing directly to the American market with a car that looked vaguely . . . American. Unsurprisingly, the USA had plenty of American-styled cars of its own, and preferred imported vehicles to have the cachet of patently European design. Sadly for Austin, this meant that the Atlantic was successful on neither side of the Atlantic – despite heroic marketing efforts that included rally outings and record attempts – and production was ended in 1952 after fewer that 8,000 of these distinctive vehicles had been built.

It's a pity, because these streamlined two-door cars are certainly appreciated (and appreciating in value) today. The first Atlantics were convertibles with an interesting optional power-operated mechanism to close the hood. A hardtop sports coupe version followed in 1949 which had an unusual wind-down rear window. In fact, the styling wasn't truly American, but did include a rounded front end with five chrome strips and central fog lamp, plus bravura touches like a 'Flying A' mascot on each wing as well as the central Austin winged motif. Those teardrop wings swept down to a sloping tail with enclosed rear wheels. It also sported novel flashing traffic indicators rather than the more usual semaphore arms and offered optional hydraulically operated windows and an Ecko radio.

But the Americans still weren't convinced, and only a few hundred were sold in the States, though buyers in Europe and British Commonwealth countries were more easily impressed and nearly half the total production run was exported to Scandinavia and Australasia. Few examples of this interesting failure have survived, as handling was poor and rust-proofing wasn't a priority.

Despite its hopeful name, the Atlantic was not a success in North America.

JUE 222

Bristol 400

When is a Bristol not a Bristol? In the case of the Bristol car company, which started production after World War II, the answer is 'when it's really a BMW'. For though the sinuous Bristol 400 touring car did indeed bear a Bristol badge, it borrowed heavily from the pre-war BMW 328, which the German company had actually exported as a rolling chassis to Britain, where it was bodied and sold by Frazer Nash.

In 1945 Frazer Nash formed a joint venture with the Bristol Aircraft Company (maker of wartime Blenheim and Beaufighter aircraft) to explore the possibility of manufacturing luxury cars. Representatives of the new consortium visited the wrecked BMW factory in Munich during 1945, 'liberating' plans and engines before the Americans managed to ship the remains of the factory's contents and machinery Stateside. BMW chief engineer Fritz Friedel was swiftly recruited to continue developing the 328 engine and a prototype was constructed in 1946. BAC gained complete control of the venture in 1947, registered the name Bristol Cars and started production of the first series Bristol 400, which was replaced by the refined second series in 1948.

The BMW heritage was significant indeed. The rear suspension replicated that of the BMW 326, the body echoed the BMW 327 and the engine and front suspension came from the BMW 328, and even the distinctive BMW twin radiator grille was incorporated. The Bristol 400's appealing aerodynamic body came in various styles. The standard saloon had bodies designed by Touring and Zagato, whilst there was a drophead styled by Farina and built at Bristol. One or two custom examples were also built, including an extraordinary 'woodie' estate car by Hyde. The long, sloping boot had a characteristic raised circular housing for the spare wheel.

FIRST MANUFACTURED:
1947 (until 1950)
ENGINE:
1,971 cc Straight Six
PERFORMANCE:
Top speed of 82 mph (132 km/h);
0-60 mph (97 km/h) in 19.7 secs
YOU SHOULD KNOW:
Developed versions of the splendid pre-war BMW 328 straight six engine would continue to power all Bristol cars until the company switched to Chrysler V8 engines in 1961.

Finders keepers - the Bristol 400 owed more than a little something to the BMW 328.

*Production of the first series
Bristol 400 started in 1947, but
just a year later a more refined
second series was released.*

Healey Sportsmobile

In the immediate aftermath of World War II Donald Healey trod the path that also attracted fellow travellers like Colin Chapman in Britain and Frank Kurtis in America – the journey from successful race driver (and accomplished automobile engineer) to manufacturer of sporty road cars. The Donald Healey Motor Company obtained a factory in Warwick and set about marrying proprietary components like Riley's proven twin cam 2.4 litre four-cylinder engine and Lockheed hydraulic brakes with a light steel box-section chassis and suspension designed and built by Healey.

Production was never prolific – the best-seller among eight different models was the 200-unit Healey Tickford Saloon of the early 1950s, whilst the Healey Elliott Saloon was the success story of the 1940s with 101 produced – but Healey's innovative cars punched far above their commercial weight by establishing a great reputation for advanced engineering, thus influencing a generation of car designers. They were all variations on the same basic mechanical package, though there were two different versions of the chassis.

The third Healey off the line was the long, low Sportsmobile, first seen in 1948 and produced until 1950, during which time very few were actually made. This four-seater drophead coupe with winding windows was built on the B chassis and is sturdy rather than handsome – with its replacement, the Abbott Drophead, definitely being more attractive to look at. Nonetheless, the Sportsmobile was a prestigious four-seater tourer that was ahead of its time, offering outstanding performance in its class.

Unfortunately, it was held back and denied the success it deserved by the British government's imposition of punitive purchase tax on all luxury cars costing more than £1,000 (when the Sportsmobile was more than double that), which badly affected Healey's sales and profitability.

FIRST MANUFACTURED:
1948 (until 1950)
ENGINE:
2,443 cc Straight Four
PERFORMANCE:
Top speed of 105 mph (164 km/h)
YOU SHOULD KNOW:
Bearing in mind that only 23 were ever made, the Healey advertising campaign for the Sportsmobile rather disingenuously stated that 'in spite of the demands of the export market a limited number of these superb cars is now available for home delivery'.

Healey Silverstone

It's a moot point whether winning rally driver Donald Healey produced road cars to subsidize his true love – racing – or whether exploits on the track were regarded as a promotional tool to boost sales of road cars. Either way, the perfect player was the magnificent Healey Silverstone, named after the wartime bomber airfield that became a racing circuit in 1948.

The Silverstone delivered the best of both worlds, making its debut in 1949 with an advertising campaign featuring glowing testimonials from leading racing drivers of the day – and yes, they really did believe in the product. This was a proven racewinner with a sizzling top speed, rapid acceleration and great roadholding at a time when there was plenty of track and hill-climbing action on offer for owner-drivers, and the Silverstone was a car that could be driven to the meet and then used to compete – and win the day.

With its rounded contours, cycle mudguards and raked windscreen (both removable if necessary to improve race performance), there can be no mistaking the fact that the Silverstone was built for speed. This cigar-shaped sports car has cutaway doors and headlamps cutely concealed behind a vertical-bar grille to accentuate that naked racing look. The Silverstone even had signature portholes borrowed from contemporary Buicks and a spare tyre jutted jauntily out of the rear end, cleverly doubling as a bumper.

Just over a hundred of these dual-purpose 'ride-and-race' sports cars were manufactured. They are regarded as the most desirable Healeys ever made and, with so few built in the two years of production, scarcity value further ups the already steep 'wow factor' price. However, these robust racers rarely vanish into static collections. They were made to be driven, and those lucky enough to have one tend to compete regularly in classic sports car races.

FIRST MANUFACTURED:
1949 (until 1950)
ENGINE:
2,443 cc Straight Four
PERFORMANCE:
Top speed of 113 mph (182 km/h); 0-60 mph (97 km/h) in 11 secs
YOU SHOULD KNOW:
Although almost all Silverstones came with Healey's enhanced 'fits everything' Riley 2.4 litre four-cylinder engine, the inevitable quest to be faster than everyone else led to a few late models being fitted with a 3.0 litre Alvis straight-six engine.

The clever doubling up of rear bumper and spare wheel was typical of Donald Healey's innovative thinking.

197

LOES V/D VELDE
MAIKEL LIESTE

The Silverstone was a proven racewinner with a sizzling top speed, rapid acceleration and great roadholding.

HRG 1500 Aero

The HRG 1500's life as a macho British roadster was cut short by World War II, but there's no keeping a good car down. No sooner had VE Day been wildly celebrated by a war-weary populace than the HRG 1500 was back, this time with a new body and impressive 'Aero' added to the name.

HRG was set up in 1936 by motor engineer Henry Ronald Godfrey (no prizes for guessing where the company name came from). Godfrey and Archie Frazer-Nash had made cycle cars together before World War I and formed a company in 1929 to supply the British forces, one notable product being the Frazer-Nash gun turret. But Godfrey also wanted to build cars for his Brooklands pals and created a wonderful 1.5 litre prototype in the best tradition of classic vintage sports cars.

FIRST MANUFACTURED:
1945 (until 1947)
ENGINE:
1,496 cc Straight Four
PERFORMANCE:
Top speed of 100 mph (161 km/h)
YOU SHOULD KNOW:
HRG also made an 1100 version of their fabled competition car, with tuned engines borrowed from Singer's Nine Tourer (the 1500 engine came from the Twelve Saloon) and, although only some 250 cars were made during two decades, their build quality may be judged by the fact that some 225 are still around.

Pre-war examples had been resolutely old-fashioned even when new – but they appealed mightily to amateurs who liked to compete in the hill-climbs and road rallies that were then popular, perhaps with the odd track excursion thrown in. They were successful too, with their low-slung, lightweight bodies and tuned engines beating almost everything on those slippery hills.

The big wheeze for the post-war world was the 1500 Aero – the old chassis with an all-new aerodynamic teardrop body dreamed up (and hammered into shape) at HRG's Surrey factory. It outshone its spartan predecessor in terms of home comforts – it even had wind-up windows – but sporty buyers were dismayed by a tendency for the bodywork to shake off during hill climbs and imbalance caused by fitting the fuel tank into a front wing. Some of the 35 Aeros HRG built were returned to be fitted with the traditional body, whilst the originals became a quirky footnote in the tale of British sports cars.

The 1500 Aero appeared in 1945 as an uprated version of the pre-war HRG 1500 speedster.

Humber Hawk

The Humber car company had an illustrious history, being one of the manufacturers that produced horseless carriages in the late 19th century. By World War I, Humber was the second largest carmaker in Britain and afterwards expanded into commercial vehicle production with the acquisition of Commer. Hillman was taken over in 1928 but in 1931 Humber itself became a takeover victim as it was swallowed by the Rootes Group.

Still, Humber continued to operate at the smart end of the Rootes spectrum throughout the 1930s, and with the advent of war switched to sturdy staff cars, sturdier armoured cars and military utility vehicles. But Humber was ready to resume car production when the war ended and – in keeping with lean times – introduced the new four-cylinder Humber Hawk rather than immediately relaunching the six-cylinder Super Snipe. Despite its name, the Hawk lacked both the grace and speed of a stooping raptor – and had the dubious advantage of being a typical British car of the immediate post-war period. In truth the snazzy name fooled nobody. The new Humber was an old pre-war Hillman 14 by any other name, with a lame sidevalve engine dating back to the early 1930s.

No matter. Rationing and a general shortage of cash ensured that few consumers could afford a new car, but Humber's reputation for nicely appointed interiors and good build quality meant that plenty of bureaucrats and businessmen were happy to splash out other people's cash for this solid four-door saloon with three window lights on each side and a sunshine roof as standard. The Mk I became the Mk II in 1947, but the only noticeable difference was that the gear lever migrated from the floor to become a column change. By 1948 Humber was able to introduce the Mk III, a genuinely fresh model.

The lumbering Humber Hawk was in fact almost identical to the pre-war Hillman 14.

FIRST MANUFACTURED:
1945 (until 1949)
ENGINE:
1,944 cc Sidevalve Straight Four
PERFORMANCE:
Top speed of 65 mph (105 km/h)
YOU SHOULD KNOW:
The Hawk went on to better things after humble beginnings, continuing to evolve as a genuine premium brand within the Rootes stable – the last big revamp coming in 1957, with Series I to IVA Hawks being manufactured until Rootes finally abandoned luxury car production a decade later.

Jaguar XK 120

FIRST MANUFACTURED:
1948 (until 1954)
ENGINE:
3,442 cc DOHC Straight Six
PERFORMANCE:
Top speed of 125 mph (201 km/h)
in road trim; 0-60 mph (97 km/h)
in 10 secs
YOU SHOULD KNOW:
The best place to chase an XK 120 is
America – over three-quarters of the
production run consisted of left-hand
drive versions destined for the car's
admirers (including Humphrey Bogart
and many other Hollywood stars) in
the United States.

Having wowed sporting drivers before World War II with the SS Jaguar 100, the company (now officially named Jaguar) impressed them even more in 1948 when it introduced the fabulous XK 120. For it was positive public reaction to the sensational concept car shown at the Earls Court Motor Show that year which persuaded Jaguar chief William Lyons to put his beautiful machine into full-scale production.

The first few hundred completed in 1948 had to be hand built with aluminium bodies over ash frames, but buoyant demand saw the introduction of pressed-steel bodies early in 1949. The 'XK' stood for Jaguar's advanced 3.4 litre six-cylinder engine, which in modified form would continue in production into the 1980s. The '120' represented the top speed – exceptional performance for a road car at the time. With the windscreen removed, ceiling speed was 136 mph (220 km/h), comfortably confirming the XK 120's status as the world's fastest production car.

This streamlined speedster was eventually produced in three body styles – first an open-top roadster, with a fixed-head coupe added in 1951 and a convertible coupe available from 1953. The roadster's detachable sidescreens and canvas top stowed behind the seats whilst the windscreen could be removed and performance-enhancing aeroscreens fitted. The convertible had a hood that folded back onto the rear deck, wind-up windows and fixed windscreen. A Special Equipment (SE) version offered a tuned engine, stiffer suspension and twin exhausts.

This high performer was a natural racer, enjoying considerable track success and setting numerous speed records. Needless to say, these sublime post-war sports cars were coveted then as now, and anyone lucky enough to pilot one gets to experience the ultimate 1940s' driving experience. There's a good chance – over 12,000 were built, making the XK 120 a great British success story.

The first XK 120s were hand built, though Jaguar soon got a regular production line going to meet buoyant demand.

Land Rover Series I

From sturdy acorns mighty oaks may grow – and that's certainly what happened in the case of Land Rover. For the inspired Series I was the forerunner of a vehicle type that would reach its zenith half a century later when the SUV (Sports Utility Vehicle) became the transport of choice for millions.

Back in the aftermath of World War II the British economy was wrecked and rationing ruled, Rover's Coventry factory had been bombed and materials for consumer goods (especially cars) were in short supply. But dispensation was available for useful products, especially anything with export potential, and chief designer Maurice Wilkes used that to advantage. A surplus wartime Willys Jeep chassis and Rover P3 car engine went into a prototype that was a cross between light truck and tractor, with the PTO (power take off) feature that allowed it to drive farm machinery.

This satisfied the 'useful' requirement and production began

There are still many Series I in circulation for some off-road fun.

in 1948. Better still, buyers paid no purchase tax as this was a 'commercial' – even though the machine launched at the Amsterdam Motor Show had become less tractor-like. The clever four-wheel drive stopgap before normal car manufacture resumed was so well received that the proposed two-year production run never ended, with the Land Rover outselling revived Rover road cars.

The original Series I was so basic that window panels and a roof of metal or canvas were optional extras, but various improvements were made before the major revamp that saw the introduction of the Series II a decade later. Larger engines were fitted (including a diesel) and long- and short-wheelbase variants appeared. But the essential character remained the same and it's not hard to find a Series I for some off-road fun – nearly three-quarters of these robust workers are still chugging on.

FIRST MANUFACTURED:
1948 (until 1958)
ENGINE:
1,595 or 1,997 cc Straight Four petrol;
1,997 cc Straight Four diesel
PERFORMANCE:
Up to 65 mph (2 litre models)
YOU SHOULD KNOW:
Nobody at Rover ever actually said
it, but the message must have been
glaringly obvious to buyers of early
Series 1 Land Rovers – you can have
any colour you like as long as it's
Army-surplus green.

*The Land Rover Series I was a
rugged off-roader that beat the
ban on road-car manufacture.*

Morris Minor

Reviving the name of a 1920s' competitor to the Austin 7, Morris Motors came up with a small saloon that would turn the tables on that formidable pre-war rival, for Austin entirely failed to match the success of the Morris Minor, which thrived for over two decades following its launch at the Earls Court Motor Show in 1948 – an event that saw many of Britain's first all-new post-war cars presented to an eager public.

Later to become famous for creating the Mini, Alec Issigonis was responsible for the Minor's innovative design. It was conceived as a vehicle for the mass market at a very reasonable price for the build quality. There were three versions in Series I – two- and four-door saloons and a convertible tourer. Plans to use a flat four motor were scrapped late in the day and a straight four sidevalve was substituted. Around a quarter of a million Minors were built in under four years, with the convertible taking a third of sales.

Series II in 1952 saw the fitting of a smaller but more powerful OHV engine (from the competing Austin A30, as Austin and Morris had merged to form the British Motor Corporation). Three new body styles appeared, too – the van, pickup and Traveller with its signature wooden frame. Series II lasted until 1956.

Cosmetic modifications were made for Series III, including a further uprating of the engine and in 1961 the Morris Minor became the first British car to sell more than one million units. An even larger engine was introduced the following year but it was the beginning of the end. The 1960s saw a steadily declining sales graph until the convertible went in 1969 and the saloon in 1970. The last of the line were Travellers made in 1971. Sadly, the Minor's replacement was the eminently forgettable Marina.

The post-war Morris Minor was the first of the cars designed by innovative Alec Issigonis.

Riley RM

After a long and honourable existence as an independent manufacturer going back to the dawn of the motoring era and beyond (starting with bicycle manufacture), the various Riley companies went bust in the 1930s. Despite producing the successful Brooklands racing car in the late 1920s and early 1930s, together with a range of attractive road cars, Riley was subsumed into the Nuffield Organisation before World War II.

But the marque remained alive and in 1945 new RM Rileys appeared, though engines were unchanged from the company's robust pre-war models. These were to be the company's last independently produced cars, though the name lived on in subsequent corporate offerings from the British Motor Corporation (BMC). The RM series consisted of the RMA (later RME) saloon, the larger RMB (later RMF) saloon and the delightful and rare RMC (a convertible RMB) and RMD (a drophead coupe). There were two wheelbase lengths, the shorter to take Riley's famous 1.5 litre engine and the longer for the 2.5 litre 'Big Four'. The last of the 'real' Rileys was the Riley Pathfinder, which superseded the RMF.

That sounds like a lot of different vehicles, but actually the family resemblance is close and the flowing lines of these fine motor cars make them instantly recognizable today. The RMs, with sturdy chassis and ash-framed bodywork, were among the last traditional British cars to be made in reasonably large quantities. Steering was by a precise rack-and-pinion system and the front suspension was wishbone and torsion bar. The interior was comfortable and well appointed, whilst handling was good and performance brisk. These attributes made the RM series popular in the 1940s and early 1950s – and extremely desirable to classic car buffs today – but sadly the era of the quality hand-built car was drawing to a close, taking Riley with it.

FIRST MANUFACTURED:
1945 (until 1955)
ENGINE:
1,496 cc or 2,443 cc Straight Four
PERFORMANCE:
Varied by model, but the RMB could reach 90 mph (145 km/h) and accelerate from 0-60 mph (97 km/h) in 16.8 secs
YOU SHOULD KNOW:
There is a very active Riley RM owners' club in Britain that stages annual rallies, often at impressive 'stately home' locations like Sandringham, where it's possible to secure a ride (and perhaps even a drive) in one of these enduring classics.

Well built and with good performance, the RM remains a firm favourite at modern British classic car rallies.

Rolls-Royce Silver Dawn

At last the days of custom-bodied Rolls-Royces were (nearly) over. The introduction of the Silver Dawn at the end of the 1940s marked the arrival of the company's first model to be sold with a standard steel body – though 64 'escaped' to be fitted with coachbuilt bodies and these are the most desirable Silver Dawns, especially soft tops like the drop-dead-gorgeous Park Ward convertible coupe. This at least confirms one traditional virtue – there was a separate chassis (riveted until 1953, welded thereafter) capable of taking either standard steel or hand-built bodies.

To reflect the hard times Britain's post-war economy was experiencing, the first Silver Dawns to emerge from the Crewe factory were left-hand drive cars destined for export. Not until the R type arrived in 1953 would these fine cars be available to home buyers. Whisper it if you dare, but the Silver Dawn was actually a Bentley with a Rolls-Royce radiator, bonnet and badge. At least Rolls-Royce was moving with the times by standardizing components between its luxury marques.

Rolls and Bentley cars saw the introduction of standardized production between the two marques with the appearance of the handsome Silver Dawn.

Not only were Silver Dawn bodies standard production numbers that had much in common with the Bentley Mk VI, but the chassis was also shared with the Bentley Mk VI (until 1952, when the R chassis was shared by both).

Unfortunately, the great export plan was undermined by one fatal flaw – the Silver Dawn had a manual column gear change and this simply wasn't good enough for the vital American market where wealthy buyers expected (and were only willing to pay for) automatic transmission. The fault was finally remedied with the introduction of an automatic version in 1953, but by then the damage was done – only 761 Silver Dawns were ever built.

FIRST MANUFACTURED:
1949 (until 1955)
ENGINE:
4,257 cc or 4,566 cc Straight Six
PERFORMANCE:
Top speed of 94 mph (151 km/h);
0-60 mph (97 km/h) in 15.2 seconds.
YOU SHOULD KNOW:
Thanks to inexperience with pressed-steel bodywork, coupled with the poor quality of post-war materials available to car makers, the legendary Rolls-Royce build quality was somewhat compromised and (shock, horror!) Silver Dawns were prone to serious rust problems.

The 1949 P4 was the first model in a range that would retain this unmistakable shape for many years to come.

Rover P4 75 'Cyclops'

The maker of the Victorian Rover Safety bicycle started producing motor cars at the dawn of the 20th century and became one of the most famous – and enduring – names in the pantheon of British motor manufacturers. Rover moved up market in the 1930s, and maintained its appeal to middle-class motorists after World War II. But in common with many cars on both sides of the Atlantic, the old-fashioned Rover P3 of 1948 was very much a pre-war revival that filled the gap before new models could be introduced.

When it came, the Rover P4 four-door saloon was mould-breaking. The modern styling had more than a hint of new-fangled American streamlining about it. Indeed, the P4 owed more than a little something to the contemporary Studebaker Champion, two examples of which had been studied closely at the Rover works. This audacious piracy was not to everyone's taste but time would tell – the ongoing P4 series lasted for 15 years and became a firm favourite with the conservative target market.

The 'P4' was actually a factory designation not in popular use. Owners would normally have referred to their 'Rover 75', but the P4 75 quickly acquired the nickname 'Cyclops' for a fog lamp mounted on the radiator grille (ironically, this feature was soon dropped as it interfered with cooling). The engine came from the Rover P3, but the addition of twin carburettors improved performance.

Around 33,000 original P4 75s were sold, though when the evolution 60s, 75 Mk IIs, 80s, 90s, 95/110s, 100s and 105R/105Ss were added the grand total for the P4 series was over 130,000 units. With all those different models, it might be assumed that there was considerable change during the life of the evolving P4, but in fact that iconic design remained virtually unaltered to the end.

FIRST MANUFACTURED:
1949 (until 1954)
ENGINE:
2,106 cc Straight Six
PERFORMANCE:
Top speed of 85 mph (137 km/h);
0-60 mph (97 km/h) in 21.6 secs
YOU SHOULD KNOW:
The Rover P4 75 chassis and engine were used by two ex-Rover engineers to create the two-seater Marauder sports car – but they failed to make a success of it and only 15 roadsters and coupes were actually produced in two years from 1950 before the chastened would-be entrepreneurs rejoined Rover.

Sunbeam Talbot 90

For those enamoured of well-built British cars, there couldn't be a better example of a post-war sports tourer. In 1948 the Sunbeam Talbot 90 was launched by the Rootes Group amidst considerable fanfare. Tuned 90s were subsequently entered into various rallies to garner valuable publicity – with notable success. Actually the car was very popular with the buying public anyway, for its innate build quality. There was a rather pallid junior version of the 90 that wasn't, lasting just two years (the Sunbeam Talbot 80, with a Hillman Minx engine).

But the 90 went on to become an established success story. The last of the Sunbeam Talbots was a solid, graceful car built on a massively strong chassis using many Humber components. The body was a modern four-door saloon envelope with vertical grille, sweeping front wings, flat sides and a nicely rounded shape. In keeping with a habit caught from America, the early models had a column gear change, though a floor change and overdrive option appeared later. This was a stable, well-behaved vehicle with excellent road manners.

The Mk I with its none-too-impressive sidevalve engine derived from a pre-war Humber came with the choice of the saloon or a pleasing two-door drophead coupe. Upgrades were made to the Mk II, which appeared in 1952. A larger overhead-valve engine was fitted and the somewhat basic suspension was much improved. Twin air inlets appeared on each side of the radiator grille and the headlights were raised.

The final revamp came in 1952 with the Mk IIA, whose tuned engine and higher top speed required bigger brakes, which were cooled by pierced wheels. Around 20,000 of these upstanding machines were manufactured, so there's always a chance of enjoying a rewarding spin in this great post-war British classic.

FIRST MANUFACTURED:
1948 (until 1954)
ENGINE:
1,944 cc or 2,267 cc Straight Four
PERFORMANCE:
Top speed of 85 mph (137 km/h);
0-60 mph (97 km/h) in 20.2 secs
YOU SHOULD KNOW:
Although production of the Sunbeam Talbot 90 officially ceased in 1954, it effectively continued for another three years in the near-identical form of the Mk III, which carried a Sunbeam Supreme badge.

The Talbot 90 was a fine British car that enjoyed rally success in the post-war years.

*The Talbot 90 was very popular
with the buying public for its
innate build quality.*

The quirky Roadster was one of several cars that were killed off (at least in part) by the high purchase tax levied on big cars.

Triumph Roadster

How do you challenge a fabulous machine like the SS Jaguar 100? That was the question facing Sir John Black of the Standard Motor Company, who assumed the awesome Jaguar would be back after World War II (he was right, though sadly for him the resulting XK 120 was even better than its predecessor). Still, Black's hopeful answer was to task the newly acquired Triumph Motor Company with the job of producing a competitor. The plans that emerged were to evolve into the post-war Triumph Roadster which – though it never did manage to be any sort of competition for the new Jaguar – has become a classic in its own right.

Retro styling harked back unapologetically to those great 1930s' coachbuilt classics, and the 1800 was launched at the Earls Court Motor Show in 1947. A bench seat was designed to accommodate three (necessitating a column change) whilst two more could perch on the rear dickey (reached via a step on the back bumper). This pair was protected by a folding windscreen, but forever remained outside the Roadster's folding soft top. The car's sweeping front wings were slightly bulbous and the headlamps appeared to hang in midair, whilst the grille was set well back from the front bumper. All of which added up to a very attractive – but unsuccessful – car.

The 1800 was succeeded by the 2000 Roadster with its larger engine, but the old-fashioned styling that so appeals to modern taste was not much appreciated in the early 1950s, when people were looking forward to an exciting new 'you've never had it so good' world. Coupled with the ruinous level of purchase tax on larger cars, this sentiment killed the Roadster in 1949. Sadly, this child of the 1930s born in the 1940s never got the chance to grow up.

FIRST MANUFACTURED:
1946 (until 1948)
ENGINE:
1,775 cc or 2,088 cc Straight Four
PERFORMANCE:
1800 – top speed of 75 mph
(121 km/h); 0-60 mph (97 km/h)
in 34.4 secs
2000 – top speed of 77 mph
(124 km/h); 0-60 mph (97 km/h)
in 27.9 secs
YOU SHOULD KNOW:
Jersey detective Bergerac managed to drive one of these handsome cars on TV, but emulating him isn't easy. Only some 2,500 1800s and a symmetrical 2,000 2000s were made and those that survive are jealously guarded by besotted owners.

Triumph Mayflower

'The Watch Charm Rolls-Royce' sounds impressive, but what a name to live up to. Sadly, the car in question didn't. The Triumph Mayflower was a post-war curiosity, with its side-valve engine and angular bodywork. This was a conscious attempt to produce a luxury small car that would ring up valuable American sales. There was a rapid increase in US car production as the 1950s loomed but demand still exceeded supply and a willingness to take wafer-thin profits in exchange for desirable dollars made British exporters competitive.

The Mayflower was conceived to exploit this situation, with a resonant name boldly borrowed from American history. And knife-edge styling was intended to put potential transatlantic buyers in mind of coachbuilt luxury cars like the Rolls-Royce that were so prestigious in the USA – though by way of insurance lip service was paid to the envelope style that had become all the rage in the late 1940s, with integral headlamps and flowing wings.

Unfortunately, despite positive press coverage following the Mayflower's launch at the 1949 Earls Court Motor Show, it was not a happy marriage. The car had a reasonable trim level but was woefully underpowered, had an awkward gearbox and rolled dramatically when cornering at anything near its modest maximum speed. Unsurprisingly, Americans hated it and Triumph threw in the towel after four painful years.

The world was then (and is now) sharply divided between a minority who love the Mayflower and those who believe it is the ugliest car ever made – the latter cruelly suggesting that 34,000 were sold only because there was such a shortage of cars that a soapbox with a lawnmower engine would have sold well. There's one positive aspect to this polarized thinking – the Mayflower is a very affordable entry-level classic car for weekend drivers, especially those who can't afford a real Roller.

FIRST MANUFACTURED:
1949 (until 1953)
ENGINE:
1,247 cc Straight Four
PERFORMANCE:
Top speed of 63 mph (101 km/h)
YOU SHOULD KNOW:
Despite aiming squarely at the American market, Triumph actually managed to ship more Mayflowers to relatively undeveloped Sri Lanka (then Ceylon) than they ever managed to sell in the United States.

The Mayflower had a striking body shape, but the poor engine and bad engineering ensured that the car was a notable flop.

Wolseley 6/80

The Wolseley Motor Company wasn't particularly fast out of the starting gate when British car production resumed after World War II, sharing the problems of all manufacturers when it came to obtaining raw materials. When the first post-war Wolseleys were finally rushed into production, two models were launched at the Earls Court Motor Show, both based on Morris cars. They were built alongside the Morris Oxford at the Morris Motor Company's Cowley factory, Wolseley having been a Morris subsidiary since 1927. The smaller of the two new Wolseleys was the 4/50, whilst the larger was the 6/80 (strictly speaking, the Six Eighty) – these designations being a combination of the number of cylinders and the horsepower of each.

The Wolseley 6/80 was well equipped and looked impressive. It had an unmistakably Morris-style rounded rear end, but the front sported an upright Wolseley grille that was very different. Yet there

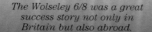

The Wolseley 6/8 was a great success story not only in Britain but also abroad.

was more than a radiator to differentiate the 6/80 from its Morris Six clone. The six-cylinder engine sported twin SU carburettors and there was a four-speed gearbox operated by a column change. The enhancements added up to lively performance and these sturdy 6/80s were used extensively as police cars, as anyone familiar with the numerous black-and-white British crime films made as supporting features in the post-war era will know.

As the Nuffield organization's luxury model, the Wolseley 6/80 benefitted from enhancements like leather upholstery, a wooden dash and door cappings, carpeting throughout, rear courtesy lights, twin fog lights, built-in reversing lamp and a red warning light inside the boot lid. The Wolseley 6/80 was a great success story. Over 25,000 were made, with nearly a third going abroad (mostly to Australia) to earn vital export revenue for Britain. The Wolseley 6/90 replaced it in 1954.

FIRST MANUFACTURED:
1948 (until 1954)
ENGINE:
2,215 cc Straight Six
PERFORMANCE:
Top speed of 85 mph (138 km/h);
0-60 mph (97 km/h) in 21.4 secs
YOU SHOULD KNOW:
Regrettably, despite widespread use as a police car, the Wolseley 6/80 had an unfortunate habit of running hot and consuming its own exhaust valves after being driven hard, thus tending to spend too much time in the MRD (Motor Repair Depot).

1950s

AC Ace

FIRST MANUFACTURED:
1953 (until 1963)
ENGINE:
1,991 CC, 1,971 CC or 2,553 CC
Straight Six
PERFORMANCE:
Top speed of 103 mph (166 km/h);
0-60 mph (97 km/h) in 11.4 secs
YOU SHOULD KNOW:
Even as it was developing and
manufacturing high-powered cars
after World War II, AC's bread-and-
butter line was a single-seat invalid
carriage with a BSA motorcycle engine
– a lucrative government contract that
would last until the mid-1970s.

AC Cars (originally Auto Carriers) was one of the first independent car manufacturers in Britain. But the company went bust at the end of the 1920s and production did not get going again until the mid-1930s. Following World War II, AC bounced back with a new 2 litre model that was traditionally built using an underslung chassis and ash-framed, aluminium bodywork offered in saloon and drophead form.

The revitalized company prospered and the impressive AC Ace roadster appeared in 1953. This had a chassis designed by John Tojeiro and was initially fitted with an evolution version of the elderly AC six-cylinder engine that had first come off the drawing board just after World War I (and would remain in production until 1963). The Ace's light weight made it a potent performer – but racing driver Ken Rudd soon fitted his own competition car with a smaller but more powerful engine derived from the pre-war BMW straight six motor subsequently developed by Bristol.

In 1957, this superior combination was put into production as the AC Ace-Bristol and enjoyed considerable track success, including creditable outings in the punishing Le Mans 24 race in 1957 and 1958. The original AC engine remained an option, but in 1961 Bristol stopped producing engines and this time the ever-inventive Ken Rudd suggested using a Ford Zephyr engine. Unfortunately, this wasn't easy, as it involved a chassis modification and redesigned front end. But the result was sensational, with many regarding the AC Ace 2.6 as the best ever. It could certainly shift, with a top speed of 125 mph (201 km/h), though sadly for lovers of macho sports cars only 37 were made.

Other variations on the 'Ace' theme included the Aceca closed coupe unveiled in 1954 and a four-seat Greyhound built on a stretched Ace chassis.

The splendid AC Ace saw a number of different engines fitted in succession as the production run unfolded.

Aston Martin DBR1

*The DBR1 remains a potent
competitor in classic car races.*

Sliding into the car that carries the registration plate XSK 497 is to sit in
(and hopefully drive) the most valuable Aston Martin in the world – the
DBR1/2, which still participates in classic road races. The 'R' stands for
Racing, and the DBR wasn't remotely like the company's production
models, though experience gained in building them did contribute to
Aston Martin's custom-built 1950s' racers, the DB3S and the DBR1. The
latter had various incarnations with the engine, space-frame chassis and
rear transaxle specially made to be teamed with components like disc
brakes and suspension from the earlier DB3S. Five were built.

Initially, the DBR1 had a 2.5 litre engine – made for a new formula
introduced after a tragic accident at Le Mans in 1955, when Pierre
Levegh's Mercedes-Benz 300 SLR hurtled into the crowd, killing both
driver and 80 spectators in the world's worst-ever motor racing disaster.
After gearbox failure in the 1956 race, the DBR1 acquired a larger
engine in the hope of challenging the Jaguar D-types, Maserati 450Ss
and Ferrari 250s – and the car did indeed enjoy modest success in 1957.
The return of gearbox problems blighted the 1958 campaign, but all that
changed in 1959.

Ten years after he bought Aston Martin, David Brown saw a long-
held ambition fulfilled. After an engine upgrade, XSK 497 sped to victory
in the prestigious Le Mans 24 race, driven by Carroll Shelby and Roy
Salvadori. Aston Martin went on to clinch the 1959 World Sportscar
Championship by winning the final race of the series at Goodwood
when the DBR1 of Shelby, Stirling Moss and Jack Fairman triumphed.
Having reached this peak of achievement, David Brown withdrew Aston
Martin from competition and set about cashing in on the newly acquired
racetrack reputation by creating a series of superb road cars.

FIRST MANUFACTURED:
1956 (until 1959)
ENGINE:
2,493 cc or 2,992 cc DOHC
Straight Six
PERFORMANCE:
Top speed of 180 mph (290 km/h)
when slipstreaming
YOU SHOULD KNOW:
When Aston Martin clinched the 1959
World Sportscar Championship at
Goodwood the car driven by Stirling
Moss went up in flames, putting
the official pit out of commission –
privateer Graham Whitehead then
scratched his DBR1 to allow the factory
entries to refuel, Moss switched to
another car . . . and drove to victory.

Aston Martin DB4/DB4GT

The DB4 was an innovative and distinctly un-English sports car, designed by Carrozzeria Touring of Milan and manufactured in Aston Martin's recently acquired Newport Pagnell factory. Using the *superleggera* (super-light) tube frame technology pioneered by Touring, together with rack and pinion steering and a powerful new 3.7 litre engine designed by Polish engineer Tadek Marek, Aston Martin constructed a landmark car – capable of 0–100 mph (161 km/h) in a mere 21 seconds, it was the first production car to hit the ton in under 30 seconds. Altogether 1,110 DB4s were produced, in five distinct 'series' with various style changes and improvements over the course of its five-year run, of which 70 were convertibles, first introduced in 1962.

Buoyed by the success of his DBR1 in the World Sportscar Championship, Aston Martin's boss David Brown didn't hesitate to milk the DB4 for all it was worth. In 1959 he produced a beefed-up

The DB4 Zagato proved very capable of pushing Ferrari to the limit in sports car races.

GT version on a shortened wheelbase for lower weight and better handling. Only 100 DB4 GTs were produced, 25 of which were sent as rolling chassis to Zagato in Milan where talented young Ercole Spada, later to be Zagato's chief designer, was given his first gig: turning out a spin-off limited edition with which to challenge Ferrari on the race circuits.

The 1960 GT Zagato was the ultimate evolution of the DB4. Spada installed a 314 bhp engine and effectually transformed the GT from a road car that could be raced into a racing car that could be driven on the road. Is the DB4 GT Zagato the most desirable Aston Martin ever? A price tag of £3.5 million when one comes up for sale suggests it is. Only 19 are in existence so don't expect to be driving one any time soon.

FIRST MANUFACTURED:
1958 (until 1963)
ENGINE:
3,670 cc DOHC Straight Six
PERFORMANCE:
The GT Zagato had a top speed of
153 mph (246 km/h);
0-60 mph (97 km/h) in 6.1 secs
YOU SHOULD KNOW:
Four DB4 'Sanction II' cars were officially given GT Zagato status at the Milan factory in 1991 – Zagato had to disassemble an original to remind themselves of the body-building technique they had used on these iconic machines back in the early 1960s.

Austin-Healey 100

The quirky Austin A90 Atlantic gave birth to a rather attractive child, though not without a lot of help from midwife Donald Healey. For he it was who took an A90 engine and chassis as the basis for his prototype Healey 100 (that seductive figure representing the car's ability to top the 'ton') which he proudly unveiled at the Earls Court Motor Show in 1952. The owner of the parent Austin Atlantic, BMC, was so impressed with Healey's streamlined roadster that it decided to sponsor a production run.

The attractive Austin-Healey 100 was a hit at the 1952 Motor Show in London, leading to a production deal with BMC.

The BN1 model that resulted was built by Jensen Motors at West Bromwich and finished at BMC's Longbridge plant in Birmingham. The BN1 had a well-tuned A90 engine and drivetrain with modified manual transmission – a three-speed box with overdrive on second and top gears. There was independent front suspension and Girling drum brakes were fitted all round. These classics with their fold-flat windscreens and clean-cut lines with few embellishments hit the market in the summer of '53 and proved to be a popular buy, vindicating BMC's decision to back Donald Healey's vision. Better still, the Austin-Healey 100 sold well in America, establishing the marque as a serious contender in the international sports car market.

The BN2 appeared in 1955, offering a four-speed gearbox, new rear axle and a choice of natty paint jobs – for the first time including a two-tone option. To satisfy those sporty buyers who wanted extra performance, a modified 100M version was created. This could be distinguished by its louvred bonnet (complete with strap). A small number of aluminium-bodied 100S (for Sebring) cars were also made. These lightweight speedsters were the most powerful 100s of all, and the first production cars in the world to have disc brakes front and back.

FIRST MANUFACTURED:
1953 (until 1957)
ENGINE:
2,660 cc Straight Four
PERFORMANCE:
Top speed of 106 mph (171 km/h);
0-60 mph (97 km/h) in 11.2 secs
YOU SHOULD KNOW:
The final '100' models became 100-6s with the fitting of a smaller straight six engine and were the 2+2 BN4 of 1956 and the two-seater BN6 of 1958. These were marginally slower than the original four-cylinder 100s but offered better acceleration.

Austin-Healey Sprite

Buoyed by the success of the Austin-Healey 100, partners BMC and Donald Healey came up with a clever new concept. The innovative 1958 Austin-Healey Sprite was designed to appeal to increasing numbers of youngsters with good incomes who were excited by the notion of open-top motoring but couldn't afford the expensive roadsters driven by their well-heeled elders. It proved to be an inspired idea.

This time the Sprite's major 'donor' was Austin's well-proven A35, with help from the Morris 1000. The engine acquired twin carburettors and the body was simplicity itself, with no external boot access or door handles. Trim was minimal and the one fancy element – pop-up headlights set into the bonnet lid – was soon abandoned as too complicated. However, fixed headlights substituted, giving this neat little sports car its characteristic appearance and quickly earning it the nickname 'Frogeye Sprite' ('Bugeye' in America). The front end, wings and all, was hinged to fold forward and give access to the engine compartment. This was also the first production sports car to use integrated construction where body panels provide the vehicle's structural strength.

These nippy little cars were ideal competition material and were campaigned by the BMC Competition Department, almost immediately securing a class win at the 1958 Alpine Rally. Many privateers appreciated the Sprite's competitive qualities and the ultimate development was the Sebring Sprite built by Williams & Pritchard under the direction of rally champion John Sprinzel. This was accepted by the FIA (Fédération Internationale de l'Automobile) as a separate model in its own right.

Many Sprites are still driven for pleasure or in competition today, maintaining that early intention that they should be the most accessible of sports cars. The early 'Frogeyes' are considered more desirable than later Mk II, III and IV evolutions with more conventional styling.

FIRST MANUFACTURED:
1958 (until 1961)
ENGINE:
948 cc Straight Four
PERFORMANCE:
Top speed of 83 mph (133 km/h);
0-60 mph (97 km/h) in 20.5 secs
YOU SHOULD KNOW:
MG with their Midget subsequently imitated the 'junior sports car' idea and the two junior sports cars are referred to collectively as 'Spridgets' (both were built at the MG factory in Abingdon). Triumph also jumped on the bandwagon with their 1962 Spitfire.

Any idea why the Sprite was nicknamed 'The Frogeye'?

Austin-Healey 3000

The 'Big Healey' appeared in 1956 when the 100-6 was introduced, continuing in production for a dozen years. The name was coined to differentiate between large and small Austin-Healeys after the Frogeye Sprite appeared, applying retrospectively to the 100-6 as well as the Austin-Healey 3000 that superseded it (with the number of cylinders replaced by cubic capacity to distinguish old from new as both models looked almost identical).

The 3000 Mk I had a larger engine than its predecessor and was built between 1959 and 1961. The BN7 version was an open two-seater and the BT7 a hardtop 2+2. Equipped with twin SU carburettors, the 3000 had Girling front disc brakes. The signature wire wheels were extra, as was the popular two-tone paint finish.

The Mk II (1961-1963) saw the fitting of triple carbs (soon dropped) with cosmetic changes like a new front grille. The BJ7 was introduced, featuring wind-up windows and a curved windscreen, though just two (trouble-free) carburettors. From 1963 the Mk III BJ8 – the most powerful and well-trimmed of all Big Healeys – was the only option. This 2+2 had a walnut-veneered dashboard, proper windows and servo-assisted brakes all round.

So much for the rugged road cars, of which over 40,000 were made – a great success story at a time when a coveted 3000 cost double the annual salary a university graduate might expect. But that's only half the story. The Austin-Healey 3000 became a famed competitor on top racing circuits around the world, such as Le Mans and the Sebring International Raceway in Florida. Works versions of the 3000 were fitted with aluminium bodywork whilst privateers devised numerous performance-enhancing modifications, and large numbers still compete in classic sports car races. The Austin-Healey 3000 remains ultra-desirable, lasts well and still drives beautifully.

FIRST MANUFACTURED:
1959 (until 1967)
ENGINE:
2,912 cc Straight Six
PERFORMANCE:
Top speed of the Mk I BT7 was 115 mph (185 km/h) with 0-60 mph (97km/h) in 11.7 secs
YOU SHOULD KNOW:
After Donald Healey parted company with British Leyland in 1966, he went on to become Chairman of Jensen Motors, where (among other achievements) he produced the Jensen-Healey to fill the void left by the Austin-Healey 3000's discontinuation.

The Austin-Healey 3000 is generally regarded as the most desirable of the great British post-war sports cars.

Each and every one of the high-performance Continentals was custom bodied by one of the UK's leading coachbuilders.

Bentley S1 Continental

When the Bentley marque enjoyed a healthy revival after World War II, parent company Rolls-Royce was heavily into badge engineering – the Bentley S1 was identical to the Silver Cloud I, with no more that the distinctive R-R radiator distinguishing the two luxury cars. They both used the same six-cylinder engine and had a four-speed automatic gearbox (though a manual one was available until 1957).

This duopoly also represented the first standardization of pressed steel body styles by Rolls, but as far as the S1 went that was far from the whole story. The vast majority of S1s were indeed factory-built saloons, but around 150 escaped to receive the distinctive accolade of handcrafted bodywork, whilst a dozen long-wheelbase versions were also custom bodied. The tale didn't end there, for six months after the S1 appeared in 1955 the Continental made its debut. This featured a tuned engine and other performance tweaks enabling Bentley to claim that the company's new speedster – helped by a switch to lightweight aluminium bodywork – was the world's fastest production car.

None of the Continentals (431 were built) were factory bodied, which led to the creation of some exquisite body shapes and showed that the great British tradition of fine coachbuilding was alive and in rude health. The likes of Hooper, H J Mulliner, Park Ward and James Young produced some to-die-for S1 Continentals that included stunning two-door fastbacks, two-door saloons, dropheads and four-door sports saloons. Quite a number of these were left-hand drive cars destined for wealthy admirers in the United States. Even Italy's famous Pininfarina got in on the act with a distinctive fastback coupe.

The Continentals may represent the crown jewels, but with only 3,538 S1s produced each and every survivor is a cherished classic that offers serious bragging rights and is still a stately drive.

FIRST MANUFACTURED:
1955 (until 1959)
ENGINE:
4,887 cc F-head Straight Six
PERFORMANCE:
Top speed of around 120 mph
(192 km/h); 0-60 mph (97 km/h)
in 12.9 secs
YOU SHOULD KNOW:
When Rolls-Royce built something it was meant to last, and the engine that went into the Bentley S1 was the final evolution of the R-R straight-six motor that had been introduced in 1922 to power the Rolls-Royce Twenty series.

Bentley S2 Continental

The super S2 Continental
confirmed that classic British
custom coachbuilders were
alive and well – just.

The Bentley Continental S1 had done well for Rolls-Royce – as did the companion Silver Shadow I – but times they were a-changing. In particular, the bell tolled for the venerable straight-six F-head, for Rolls introduced a 6.2 litre aluminium V8 that immediately went into uprated Bentley S2s and Rolls-Royce Silver Cloud IIs.

These powerful grand tourers were ideal for their era. Motorways, autoroutes, autobahns and autostrada were proliferating all over Europe with speed limits no more than a cloud on the horizon. The large, heavy S2 was more than capable of taking full advantage, cruising at high speed for hours on end – an attribute appreciated by wealthy owners and envied by drivers of most contemporary mass-produced cars. But the new engine was teamed with an old-fashioned chassis and servo-assisted drum brakes (at least now boasting four shoes) reminiscent of the Edwardian era. It would not be long before the S3 arrived to address some of those deficiencies.

In the meantime, that old-fashioned chassis allowed the S2's Continental derivative to enjoy the stylish addition of hand-build custom bodywork, though creative coachbuilders were coming under pressure from the rise and rise of monocoque construction. But they could still deliver the goods. H J Mulliner offered traditional elegance, producing the famous 'Flying Spur' – a six-light design considered to be one of the most handsome large saloons ever. Mulliner was equally at home with the two-door coupe, though Park Ward specialized in attractive fixed and drophead coupes and other coachbuilders like James Young gatecrashed the Continental party.

The S-series would be the last real opportunity for these superb coachbuilders to strut their stuff, and the S2 Continentals are regarded as the best of the best – having more power and flexibility than S1s without the added weight of S3s.

FIRST MANUFACTURED:
1959 (until 1962)
ENGINE:
6,230 cc OHV V8
PERFORMANCE:
Top speed of 120 mph (185 km/h); 0-60 mph (97 km/h) in 11.4 secs
YOU SHOULD KNOW:
Rolls-Royce could have its cake and eat it with the S2 Continental – for both the coachbuilder entrusted with creating the closed bodies (H J Mulliner) and the company tasked with developing the open bodies (Park Ward) were actually owned by Rolls-Royce.

Daimler SP250 (Dart)

Launched in New York as the Dart, Daimler's first sports car was officially renamed the SP250 after Dodge claimed copyright. The car was a barefaced attempt to ride the wave of popularity for British sports cars in America, and it looked much more transatlantic than the Triumph or MG competitors on which its chassis was based. Daimler's boldness, and hurry to enter the market, resulted in confused styling. From the front, the fibreglass moulded lines curl sinuously down to the wide grille. From the rear three-quarter view, the futuristic horizontal and vertical lines forming the SP250's outrageous fins seem to belong to another car.

Even so, the awkward design looks sexy – but it is the authoritative throaty rumble from the SP250's twin exhausts that confirms it. Powered by a 2.5 litre V8 engine, the SP250 is a joy to

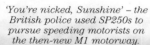

'You're nicked, Sunshine' – the British police used SP250s to pursue speeding motorists on the then-new M1 motorway.

drive. Once initial problems of the chassis (the doors on the original 'A' spec version had a tendency to fly open on tight bends) had been ironed out, the car began to fulfil its destiny as a two-door, open-topped king of the road. It was, and is, fun. Its responsive acceleration appeals as strongly to enthusiasts as it once did to the British police, who fielded a number of automatic versions as high-speed pursuit vehicles.

The real surprise is that Daimler ever made the SP250 (Dart). For decades the company had been associated firmly with upmarket family saloons and limited production of luxury limousines (whose clientele included the British Royal Family). The SP250 is really a delightful aberration. Its oddity, as well as its success, marks it as a product of a very specific, late 1950s' social climate.

FIRST MANUFACTURED:
1959 (until 1964)
ENGINE:
2,548cc OHV V8
PERFORMANCE:
Top speed of 123mph (198 km/h);
0-60 mph (97 km/h) in 9.2 secs
YOU SHOULD KNOW:
Take a head-on look at the SP250 (Dart) engine grille, and you won't be surprised that some enthusiasts call it 'the Catfish'.

Daimler Majestic Major

FIRST MANUFACTURED:
1959 (until 1968)
ENGINE:
4,561 cc V8
PERFORMANCE:
Top speed of 120 mph (193 km/h);
0-60 mph (97 km/h) in 9.7 secs
YOU SHOULD KNOW:
Jaguar Cars purchased Daimler in
1960 and experimented by putting the
4.5 litre Daimler V8 engine from the
Majestic Major into a Jaguar
Mk X – and thus equipped the lighter
car proved capable of reaching a top
speed of 130 mph (209 km/h).

The Daimler Majestic 101 was launched in 1958, in the hope that there was still demand for a sturdy saloon in the best traditions of this famous marque. The Majestic was mechanically advanced but had a traditional coachbuilt body on a heavy chassis that made this large car hard to manoeuvre – though a lusty 3.8 litre engine meant the Majestic could sail past 100 mph (161 km/h). Barely a year after the Majestic hit the road, the Majestic Major appeared in 1959.

The two models ran concurrently until 1962 and were virtually impossible to tell apart. The difference was beneath the bonnet, where a new hemi-head V8 engine lurked. This was both lighter and more powerful than the old straight six, considerably improving the Majestic Major's performance. Ironically, more Majestics than Majestic Majors were sold, despite the fact that the former was available for five years and the latter for nearly a decade.

The Majestic Major was certainly a high-performance luxury car that could reasonably hope to attract executives who had not quite reached Rolls-Royce or Bentley status, but still liked the thought of being seen in a prestigious car. But perhaps it was stylistically old before its time, with more modern alternatives having better curb appeal for a new generation of businessmen. And despite an impressive top speed, advanced Borg Warner automatic transmission and servo disc brakes all round, this clumsy machine had a huge turning circle and power steering was not standard until 1964. It was not successful, with fewer than 1,200 built.

A stretched DR450 limousine based on the Majestic Major appeared in 1961, for those with chauffeurs and the carriage trade. It was also adapted into a hearse, many examples of which are still doing stately service today – definitely not the version you want to ride.

Launched just before the Swinging Sixties, Daimler's sturdy Majestic Major managed to look old before its time.

Ford Zephyr Mark II

The Zephyr Mk II sought to bring to Britain the American look that was all the rage.

By the middle of the 1950s Ford of Britain was reaching its industrial zenith. Success at every market level was maintained by constant innovation and improvement. With its Consul/Zephyr/Zodiac range, Ford had already struck gold in both sales and motorsport. A Mk I Zephyr (originally known as the Zephyr Six) had won the Monte Carlo Rally in 1953 and the East African Safari in 1955, enhancing the car's reputation for good value. Problems of understeer and limited performance were overcome with easily made modifications that improved handling and added as much as 20 mph (32 km/h) to the top speed.

Success bred success. In 1956 the new Mk II Consul/Zephyr/Zodiac models were acclaimed as 'the three graces', thanks to their stunningly family-friendly new lines. The Mk II Zephyr benefited most. Longer, heavier, wider and more powerful, its popularity as the biggest mass market family car was assured – considerably helped by a run of competition successes crowned by winning outright the 1959 RAC Rally.

It was the Mk II Zephyr that opened the door for Ford's later adventures with the Cortina and the Escort. Many are still competing in Classic and other events: and drivers' reports of powering a Mk II up a snowy mountain pass, or controlling the well-behaved heavyweight hurtling through mud-clogged forest lanes, continue to excite everyone who has ever dreamed of their family car transforming into a supercar. The Zephyr Mk II is the car that proves you don't have to be rich to be a winner.

FIRST MANUFACTURED:
1956 (until 1962)
ENGINE:
2,553 cc OHV Straight Six
PERFORMANCE:
Top speed of 89 mph (143 km/h);
0-60 mph (97 km/h) in 17 secs
YOU SHOULD KNOW:
A factory-modified Mk II rallying version had a top speed of over 101 mph (163 km/h) and achieved 0-60 mph (97 km/h) in less than 10 secs.

Ford Anglia 105E/123E Super

Designed to fit into an existing range of Ford cars, the Anglia 105E was all new. As a two-door, four-seater family saloon it broke completely with traditional styling. The wind-tunnel tested and streamlined smoothness of its swept-back nose and flat roof line, the muted tailfins and reverse-raked rear window (like contemporary Lincolns and Mercurys) suggested American glamour even in the standard budget version. Most people opted for the 105E Deluxe, with a full width grille, chrome side strips and rear light surrounds, and two-tone trim.

Equally exciting was the 105E engine, a gleaming 997cc OHV (overhead valve) straight four which became the basis of Ford engines

The Anglia, with its slanting rear window, had revolutionary styling for the time.

292 GCR

for many years. Easy to tune, and as 'tweakable' as the styling, the Kent engine quickly became beloved of hot-rodders. In fact the 105E was so successful that in 1962 Ford introduced the Anglia 123E Super. It had more chrome, more comfort, more power and more flash: the 105E/123E is what people mean by an Anglia. It has never been out of style. As one generation of drivers enjoyed it and moved on, another discovered its motor sport potential. It's instantly recognisable, an icon of a peculiarly British vision of modernity. Now it's loved for its retro-chic and adaptability at every level. A blue 105E featured (airborne, and magically customized to hold nine people!) in the film *Harry Potter and the Chamber of Secrets*.

FIRST MANUFACTURED:
1959 (105E); 1962 (123E) (until 1967)
ENGINE:
997cc (105E), 1,198cc (123E) OHV
Straight Four
PERFORMANCE:
Top speed of 74 mph (119 km/h)
YOU SHOULD KNOW:
In 1962 a Ford Anglia 105E was driven for seven days and nights at the Montlhery circuit near Paris, at an average speed of more than 83 mph (133 km/h). It set six new world records for a car under 1,000 cc.

Jaguar XK150

FIRST MANUFACTURED:
1957 (until 1960)
ENGINE:
DOHC Straight Six (available as 3.4/3.4S and 3.8/3.8S)
PERFORMANCE:
A 3.4 l XK150S FHC achieved a top speed of 132 mph (212 km/h) and 0-60 mph (97 km/h) in 7.8 secs.
YOU SHOULD KNOW:
What we now know as Jaguar Cars was founded in 1922 as the Swallow Sidecar Company. After World War II, the company had to change its name because of 'associations' with the initials forming its previous logo – SS.

Though Jaguar is now a subsidiary of Ford, the marque is still esteemed for its pre- and post-World War II reputation for luxury saloons and competitive sports cars. In 1948, Jaguar had thrilled the motoring world with its XK120, still sought after and enjoyed for its mean, lean, sporting lines. Nine years and the XK140 later, the company's wealth of racing and marketing experience was poured into the XK150, the last and most glamorous of its species. Obvious family resemblances were misleading: the XK150's subtly improved, but still Old World styling incorporated extensive modernization that paved the way for both the stylistic Great Statement of the E-Type and the mechanical glories of the XK engine-powered sports saloons of the 1960s.

In fact the first XK 150s were not as fast as their predecessors. Their beefed-up curves (with the new one-piece windscreen, wider bonnet and wing line raised almost to door level, the heavier car still looked as athletically poised and dangerous as the leaping mascot itself!) relied on the XK140's standard 3.4 engine. But from 1958, the 3.4 and (later) 3.8 litre versions could be tuned to 'S' form, restoring real performance to match the car's aura of stylish menace. You could have a Fixed Head Coupe (FHC), a two-to-three seater like the Drop Head Coupe (DHC), or the Roadster.

In the XK150's short production life (to October 1960), almost 10,000 owners succumbed in equal measure to the magic of the three versions. Subsequently, in his first film as actor/director, Clint Eastwood immortalized one of them in *Play Misty For Me*. In every way, the XK150 bears the hallmarks of discriminating taste: like so many Jaguars, it talks quietly, and walks the walk effortlessly, on demand.

The XK150 was the final incarnation of Jaguar's truly awesome XK sports range.

Jaguar Mark II

Jaguar hit the jackpot in 1959 when it redesigned the company's first monocoque (body and chassis as single unit) four-door saloon. The Mark II's bigger windows created an impression of airy brightness, and minor changes to the trim, instrument panel and external styling all added up to a handsome car that drivers felt to be 'adult'. It made much more of the existing 2.4 and 3.4 litre engines – but the star of the range was the new 3.8 litre version of the legendary XK. Ensconced in serious leather-and-walnut comfort (that subsequently became one of Jaguar's hallmarks), Mark II drivers discovered how easily the 3.8 could embarrass contemporary sports cars in both acceleration and speed. With a slightly wider rear axle, the improved road-handling was impeccable; and even the optional wire wheels had an additional, useful function in providing extra cooling for the now standard disc brakes.

The Mark II catapulted Jaguar into the role of style leader for sports saloons. In practice, its speed and manoeuvrability made it first choice both for old-style criminals in need of a getaway car, and for the police chasing them. Featured in lots of British films and TV shows of the early 1960s, the Mark II has always retained its image of quirky individualism. It still does. It even transcends the usual barriers of class and wealth: owners were and are just as likely to be wage-earners as aristocrats. More than fifty years after it was first launched, its unceasing popularity among connoisseurs makes the Mark II the perfect expression of its originator's (William Lyons, Jaguar's Chairman) desire to build a car of 'grace, space and pace'. Its combination of luxury and performance made it a paragon of aspirational sophistication that may have been equalled, but never surpassed.

The Jaguar Mark II was born out of a desire to build a car of 'grace, space and pace'.

FIRST MANUFACTURED:
1959 (until 1967)
ENGINE:
2,483 cc, 3,442cc, 3,781 cc DOHC
Straight Six
PERFORMANCE:
Top speed of 125 mph (201 km/h);
0-60 mph (97 km/h) in 8.5 secs
YOU SHOULD KNOW:
The Jaguar Mark II's most enduring cultural success is probably as the car driven by Inspector Morse in the internationally successful TV series based on the novels of Colin Dexter. Although the car used in the TV series was the less desirable 2.4 version, and somewhat battered, it was sold in 2005 after restoration for over £100,000.

Along with many an upwardly mobile but honest Brit, armed robbers tended to go for a speedy top-of-the-range Jaguar 3.8.

Lagonda 3.0 Litre

The Lagonda was a marque of automotive aristocracy more than equal to its luxury sports car competitors, Bentley, Invicta and Railton. When Rolls-Royce bought him out, W O Bentley in fact chose to move to Lagonda, which was acquired in 1947 by the industrialist David Brown at much the same time as Aston Martin, for whose salvation he depended on Bentley's legendary engineering. Brown put the available 2.6 litre Bentley engine first into his Aston Martin DB2, and only in 1948 into his first Lagonda, a wonderful but old-fashioned, somewhat stately magnificence. It was 1953 before he announced the new 3 litre Lagonda, powered by a revised Bentley engine capable of topping the magic 100 mph (161 km/h), and featuring the advanced design of a cruciform-braced chassis and all-round independent suspension. Initially, though seating four, it came only as a two-door closed saloon or a convertible drophead coupe (styled by the Swiss coachbuilder Graber). Though fast, the column-change gearbox detracted from its sporty appeal.

By 1954, the gear change was floor mounted, and drivers could feel they were truly participating in one of the era's great motoring experiences. The saloon appeared with four doors, and the drophead coupe just got better. You bathed in leather and walnut, with every available extra installed as standard in a vehicle of supremely discreet elegance, while the engine effortlessly dealt with the solid weight of genuine luxury. Five people could be comfortable in a 3 litre Lagonda; and even with the ample boot crammed with luggage, the car fulfilled its fastest specs.

HRH the Duke of Edinburgh thought so, too, and had his 3 litre Lagonda Drophead Coupe finished in Edinburgh Green with Battleship Grey upholstery. He even persuaded his bride, HM The Queen, to use it in 1959 on the occasion of the official opening of Britain's first motorway, the M1.

The Lagonda was a convertible drophead coupe beloved of the well-heeled British upper classes.

Lotus Elite

Its streamlined elegance flabbergasted the motoring world when it was unveiled at the London Earls Court Motor Show of 1957. The Lotus Elite's fibreglass monocoque engineering was the very first combination of its kind. It was also the first 'regular', roadgoing, production sports car created by the maverick engineering genius Colin Chapman and his team, even if the first line-produced car was not made until mid-1958 (and bought, incidentally, by the celebrated jazz musician Chris Barber). Though there was a steel subframe to support the engine, suspension and essentials like the door hinges, the Elite's featherweight and advanced aerodynamic construction balanced on four-wheel independent suspension, made it a dream to handle. It was a wonderfully fast car. In fact, to begin with, the 1.2 litre engine made it almost overpowered – but it provided the Elite with the authentic sports car performance that gained it, among many triumphs, six class victories in the Le Mans 24 hour. The interior had carefully matching, stylish practicality – including a metal dashboard shaped exactly like the Elite's exterior profile.

There were major problems. The drive was bolted directly to the monocoque without even rubber cushions. The noise was horrendous. Forget 'opening the windows': curved on two planes so they couldn't wind down into the doors, the only option was to remove them completely and stow them in special pockets behind the seats. Worse, the glass fibre bodywork was liable to crack.

Not even shifting body manufacture to the Bristol Aircraft Company resolved the Elite's shortcomings. Yet its performance belied its fragility – and when you see one today, zipping along with fluid elegance, it's impossible to forget that the Lotus Elite is a car whose subsequent influence entitles it to be universally lauded as a genuine ancestor.

The Lotus Elite was attractive, but was beauty enough to compensate for bad manners?

FIRST MANUFACTURED:
1957 (prototype); 1958 (production) (until 1963)
ENGINE:
1,216 cc Straight Four
PERFORMANCE:
Top speed of 115 mph (185 km/h); 0-60 mph (97 km/h) in 12.2 secs
YOU SHOULD KNOW:
If you enjoy automotive mathematics, investigate the Lotus Elite's incredible drag coefficient. Those gentle, delicate curves contain nothing superfluous. The Elite's beauty is dedicated to achieving its coefficient of 0.29, brilliant today, and simply unheard of in 1957.

Lotus Seven

The maverick automotive genius of Britain's Colin Chapman was in overdrive in 1957. For nearly ten years (including his RAF service) the engineering visionary had been refining increasingly successful versions of his super-lightweight sports race cars. He was close to achieving his goal of creating a Formula One contender, and every move was the subject of fascinated public scrutiny. The public loved his Lotus 6, a genuinely low-cost, street-legal competitor which they could drive to the track or hillclimb, compete, and go home in afterwards. They wanted more – and they thought they could see it in the one-off Lotus Seven fitted with a Coventry Climax engine, de Dion rear suspension and disc brakes that slaughtered the hillclimb and sprint season opposition of that year. Chapman, pressed for a

The Lotus Seven was produced by the speed-obsessed Colin Chapman as the best possible budget driver's car.

road version, gave them a prototype classic instead, still in production according to its virtually original design more than fifty years later, and the blueprint for dozens of imitators around the world.

The Lotus Seven of legend first appeared in kit form. It was a stroke of minimalist genius, using readily available parts that would fit into the radical geometry of its lightweight, tubular and steel panel frame. De Dion was ousted for the solid beam axle of a Nash Metropolitan. The tiny engine was taken from the genteel Ford Prefect and Anglia (though when it began selling complete cars in 1958, Lotus offered the Climax or the BMC 'A' series from the Austin Sprite). There were some real problems (a tendency for rust to eat into the tubular chassis, causing sudden, terrifying collapse!), and the Lotus Seven was so Spartan, unadorned and basic that it was described as 'like driving a motorized roller-skate'. Enormous fun, in fact. The Seven is about sporty performance, brilliant handling, and – all but literally – driving by the seat of your pants.

FIRST MANUFACTURED:
1957 (until 1972)
ENGINE:
1,172 cc Flathead Straight Four
PERFORMANCE:
Top speed of 85.5 mph (136.8 km/h);
0-60 mph (97 km/h) in 14.3 secs
YOU SHOULD KNOW:
Under British tax laws in 1957, you didn't have to pay Purchase Tax on a car kit as long as it did not contain assembly instructions. So Chapman included disassembly instructions which you followed in reverse – a bit of lateral thinking typical of Chapman's whole subversive ethos. In 1973 when the tax advantage loophole was plugged, Lotus sold the licence to build kits and complete Sevens to Caterham Cars.

The TD was the last in a line of MGs that offered classic pre-war styling, soon to be superseded by a more modern look.

MG TD

The traditions that dominate the evolution of MG sports cars include the company's reluctance to introduce radically new styling while its existing models still have a steady market. All kinds of technological developments might take place under the hood or in and around the chassis, but visible changes suggest annual tweaking rituals rather than re-styling ambition. MG's 'T' series was introduced in 1936. A new engine, hydraulic brakes and synchromesh on the top gears justified the new designation, but the styling was itself an evolution of the 'PB' series it replaced. Its successor (after 'TB' and 'TC') the MG TD still belonged to the same archetype of pre-war 'British-look' sports cars. It was a two-door roadster, wider and sleeker than its narrow, straight-backed forebears, but with the same big grille and sporty, flowing lines. The running boards were tweaked a little further forward as a civilizing gesture, and other changes (like the bumpers, newly mandatory in the US, MG's prime market at the time) all demonstrated MG's awareness of its customers' developing stylistic sophistication and demand for comfort. Within a few months, the MG TD Mk II included yet more improvements – but the essential driving experience remained the same.

It was fun. It was fast. It was reliable. It was a car to fall in love in (and, very often, with). With or without a passenger, it was a racer. Many owners did race – especially in the USA, which gobbled up roughly 23,500 of the 30,000 TDs ever made (only 149 right-hand drive cars were made for British buyers) – but its exhilarating road-holding and nippy characteristics were equally evident on the open road. Though an improved 'TF' followed, the 'TD' was the most popular of its series. It stands proudly on the cusp of old and new, in the place of honour.

FIRST MANUFACTURED:
1950 (until 1953)
ENGINE:
1,250 cc Straight Four
PERFORMANCE:
A 1952 road test by *Motor* magazine saw the MG TD achieve a top speed of 77 mph (123 km/h), and 0-60 mph (97 km/h) in 18.2 secs.
YOU SHOULD KNOW:
This beautiful, classic car has such a perennial hold on motoring enthusiasts' imaginations that in 1998 all manufacturing and associated rights in the MG TD were vested in TD Cars company in Malaysia, to reproduce the original as TD2000.

MG MGA

After 20 years of the highly traditional 'T' series sports car, MG appeared to break with its usual *modus operandi*. The MGA came to its public as an unknown Adonis, the first MG with a full-width body and streamlined curves. In fact, though the styling was indeed radically new, it had (as always with MG) been evolved over four years from a prototype shell based on the 'TD' series, and progressively refined. The engine was a BMC B series already chosen for the MG Magnette sports saloon. Its size meant the hood line could be lowered, reducing the drag coefficient. Mutterings about 'underpower' were stilled when the MGA (suitably handicapped) totally outperformed its predecessor and stablemate, an MG TF 1500. The MGA's stylish aerodynamics alone were shown to add just under 10 secs to its top speed.

The MGA faced the future squarely. Traditionalists were disappointed, but the company was firmly fixed on innovation and improvement. Almost immediately the engine was uprated (from 68 to 72 bhp). Then came a 'bubble-top' coupe version with the sports car luxury of wind-up windows, and the first of a procession of stylistic adjustments throughout the car's production. The Twin-Cam of 1958 looked normal, but revelled in a competitive ability to hit 114 mph (183.5 km/h) or more. In anything but expert hands, it was unreliable. In its place came the MGA 1600 Mark I & II, which did most of the same things, and stayed on their respective feet. Finally, every development was incorporated into a few, leftover, twin cam chassis and designated the MG MGA 1600 Mk II Deluxe. It was now a brilliant, beautiful, high-performance sports car (with a really snappy name!), but its time had passed. Luckily, the MGB was waiting in the wings.

FIRST MANUFACTURED:
1955 (until 1962)
ENGINE:
1,489 cc OHV Straight Four
PERFORMANCE:
Top speed of 98 mph (157 km/h);
0-60 mph (97 km/h) in 15 secs
YOU SHOULD KNOW:
Besides starring in a 1970s' Kellogs Corn Flakes commercial on Golden Gate bridge, the MGA has an excellent Hollywood pedigree. Among other films, it features in *Animal House* (1978) and *Guess Who's Coming to Dinner* (1968). Most conspicuously, Elvis Presley liked the red 1960 MGA 1600 Mk I roadster he used throughout *Blue Hawaii* (1961) so much that he bought it. You can see it at Graceland.

The unmistakable rounded grille of the MGA – first in a new generation of MG cars.

*Innovative and beautiful,
the MGA featured in many
Hollywood films.*

If one car looked to the future it was surely the brilliantly fast Mini Cooper that appeared in 1959 before accelerating into the new decade.

Mini Cooper

In 1959 the Austin/Morris Mini changed the face of motoring. Just 3 m (10 ft) long, it was the most efficient and effective use of road space ever seen. The apparent miracle of Sir Alec Issigonis's design was to create a front-wheel drive, two-door, four-seat economy saloon that sacrificed nothing to exact steering, superb handling, and super-agile response. At the time of its first launch, BMC (which included Austin and Morris, and marketed the Mini under both to keep the names before the public) lent a Mini to John Cooper, whose racing cars were then approaching the peak of their success (in several formulae, including two Formula 1 World Championships). He was immediately fascinated. By 1961 his 'idea' for a hot Mini had been researched, tested and produced – to a tidal wave of public and professional applause.

It was a social revolution as much as anything. The Mini Cooper, brilliant on the track and winner of numerous Monte Carlo Rallies, was the car of Britain's about-to-be 'swinging 60s' elite. In London the unofficial race track was Belgrave Square (there was much less traffic than today). The manic screeching of tyres at night is said only to have been tamed when a local policeman got his own Mini Cooper to give chase.

The Mini Cooper, and of course the even snappier Cooper 'S', have added to their legendary exploits with every incarnation. Like the Mini itself (and the MINI, as current owners BMW distinguish their versions), the Cooper has appeared in dozens of configurations, from economy to super-deluxe and back again. It has always guaranteed and delivered pure thrill; and that's why so many people continue to admire and drive one more than fifty years on.

FIRST MANUFACTURED:
1959
ENGINE:
997 cc Straight Four
PERFORMANCE:
Top speed of 85 mph (137 km/h); 0-60 mph (97 km/h) in 17.5 secs
YOU SHOULD KNOW:
Customized Minis or Mini Coopers were stars in films like *The Italian Job*, *A Shot In The Dark*, and the Beatles' *Magical Mystery Tour*. Owners included Steve McQueen, Enzo Ferrari, Marianne Faithfull, all four Beatles, and Peter Sellers (whose Mini had wicker side-panels designed by the Rolls-Royce coachbuilder, Hooper). The Legend continues.

Morgan 4/4

The company was famous for its three-wheelers when Morgan announced its first '4-4 – four wheels and four cylinders' cars in 1936. It returned from war production in 1950 with its Plus-4, a commercial success but a demographic step too far upmarket for the marque's core enthusiasts. So in 1955 Morgan introduced the Morgan 4/4 Series II (note the subtle change from 4-4 to 4/4) as a lower-powered, lightweight, nippy return to the company's original principles. Ever since, through succeeding generations of power plants and every kind of technical evolution, the car has existed in a category of its own.

Sturdy but light, built from aluminium on an ash frame, the Morgan 4/4 has survived many experiments in modern materials, and innumerable cycles of fashionability. In effect, the experience of providing fast, fun, recreational transport at the lowest practicable cost, to which the original Henry Morgan devoted himself in 1910, locked the company into a way of doing things which it has never been able to change without compromising the reasons for its success. Owners and drivers of the Morgan 4/4 of any era get particular pleasure from tinkering. Closed factory systems and computerized technology inhibit this, so Morgan avoids them where it can. The outward, still 1930s' styling is a hallmark of the 4/4's longstanding promise of keen handling and performance characteristics that can readily be modified to suit an individual's requirements (or expectations). The Series II, and every subsequent version, comes with all the technical mod cons of the day – but it always looks and drives like you've just roared in, rimed with dust where your goggles sheltered your eyes, from the Mille Miglia or the Indy 500, or even Box Hill. The Morgan 4/4 is, par excellence, the sports car of Everyman's imagination. That's why it's still going strong.

FIRST MANUFACTURED:
1955 (Series II) (until 1959)
ENGINE:
1,172 cc flathead Straight Four Ford 100E
PERFORMANCE:
Top speed of 75 mph (121 km/h);
0-60 mph (97 km/h) in 26.9 secs
YOU SHOULD KNOW:
You get a very direct ride in a Morgan 4/4, but the car has never been built for raw power. Its success is the result of decades of cunning, balancing the least available power to the least available structural weight.

The ash frames of Morgans have always been produced using traditional hand-crafted methodology, and they still are.

The classic 1950s' Riley 1.5 couldn't quite make up its mind what it was supposed to be.

Riley 1.5

Throughout the 1930s and 1940s Riley was numbered among Britain's most successful manufacturers of sports cars, sporting saloons, and even luxury limousines. Their characteristic, slightly raffish and aristocratic styling did not survive the 1952 merger of the Nuffield group (including Riley) with Austin, which formed BMC. It took five years for the merger to bear fruit: twin replacements for the Morris Minor 1000, to be launched as the Wolseley 1500 and then, later, the Riley 1.5.

It was a radical change for the Riley. Fifty years of sporting elegance were replaced by a four-door, mid-size family saloon on which awkward curves vied uncomfortably with straight lines. The Riley 1.5 looked like it couldn't decide if it wanted to look American, or just a little like a Jaguar, if only by its suggestive grille shape. It was safe, solid, comfortable, and at least it was more powerful than the Wolseley, with which it shared so many Morris Minor components. Both were fitted with the BMC B-series engine, but the Riley's twin SU carburettors gave it substantially more clout. It also had some of the same attention to interior detail of its more magnificent Riley predecessors, like the walnut veneer and extensive dial arrangement of the fascia.

The Riley 1.5 was successful enough to warrant a Mark II version, an almost entirely cosmetic style-tweak that enabled it to be sold in a sporty duo-tone version; and in 1961, a Mark III, with lower suspension. In fact, BMC's Australian-built Riley 1.5s incorporated more changes than were ever made in Britain. In its place of origin, the Riley 1.5 is a monument to motoring decency. Impeccably behaved, and both comfortable and speedy, it belongs neither to the past nor the future. It's in the middle.

FIRST MANUFACTURED:
1957 (until 1965)
ENGINE:
1,489 cc Straight Four
PERFORMANCE:
Top speed of 84 mph (135 km/h);
0-60 mph (97 km/h) in 24.8 secs
YOU SHOULD KNOW:
The Riley 1.5 had a high final drive in the axle, which meant it could cruise comfortably at speed. For a small car, it also proved surprisingly lively in contemporary races and rallies. Its Riley ancestors would have approved.

Rolls-Royce Silver Cloud II

The Rolls-Royce Silver Cloud II is the last of the illustrious marque of which the motoring world could agree: 'This is the best car in the world'. It performed better than any previous Rolls-Royce; and every model that followed (starting with the re-styled Silver Cloud III) marked a further compromise on a long road to relative mediocrity.

The Cloud II shared its fabulous grandeur with Cloud I. There were minor cosmetic changes, but only in the cause of technical improvement or greater luxury, like the improved headlights and the addition of adjustable fresh air vents to the fascia. Cloud II also had more body styles, adding a two-door convertible and two-door coupe to the range. Like Cloud I, Cloud II had the 'standard steel' sedan body, its mighty wings rolling backwards in a wave of refined elegance to meet their rear echo, and every subtle curve and scoop in harmony with the whole. As always with Rolls-Royce, there were long-wheelbase limousines (299 of 2,417) with handcrafted coachwork and a division window, but the Crewe standard was an international hallmark of complete excellence.

The Silver Cloud II took that excellence to new technical heights. It was the first Rolls-Royce to be powered by a V8. With or without General Motors' excellent automatic transmission (R-R and Bentley had used it for years), Cloud II was faster, quieter, accelerated much better, and now had power steering as standard to make it much easier to handle and respond. The only faults you could possibly find with it are retrospective: in its day, high fuel consumption was not an issue, and if the chassis or bodywork proved prone to rust fifty years later, frankly, big deal. It's the only car that feels as good to be driven in as it does to drive.

FIRST MANUFACTURED:
1959 (until 1962)
ENGINE:
6,230 cc V8
PERFORMANCE:
Top speed 117 mph (188 km/h);
0-60 mph (97 km/h) in 10.8 secs
YOU SHOULD KNOW:
The Rolls-Royce Silver Cloud is the car which prompted the immortal advertising slogan 'At 60 miles an hour, the loudest noise in this new Rolls-Royce comes from the electric clock'.

Elegant, fast, comfortable and quiet, the Silver Cloud II proved a hit with both drivers and passengers.

*How else could the good and
the great possibly get around?*

The TR2 was a very successful combination of assorted components that included a pre-war Standard chassis and a modified Ferguson tractor engine.

Triumph TR2

The Triumph TR2 was a triumph of willpower. The forerunner of one of Britain's most successful sports car series, it was created by Sir John Black, head of the Standard Motor Company and of Triumph. Standard had supplied engines to the fledgling Jaguar Company, and Black desperately wanted to share or compete with Jaguar's success. His first efforts, the Triumph 1800 and Triumph 2000, were classic British sports cars, but already stylistically outmoded. Then Jaguar pre-empted his plans with the fabulous XK120. The ingenious Sir John spotted a gap in the market. Necessity for strict economy in development and production drove the inspired invention of a truly beautiful, small open roadster. It hit the bullseye.

The TR2's witches' brew of components defied identification in the glorious finished product. The new car was based on unused frames from the pre-war Standard Flying Nine. The engine was devised from the 2.1 litre four used in both the Standard Vanguard and the Ferguson tractor. The suspension and rear axle came from the Triumph Mayflower sedan (you couldn't make this up!). To save costs on stamping compound curves, the panels were beaten and welded; and the depth of the front intake hid a simple mesh instead of a formal grille. The designers even abandoned their idea for retractable headlight pods, and installed the fixed pods that completed the TR2's 'frog-eye' front.

For something out of nothing, the TR2 was a tour de force. America loved it, too, and the car won many Sports Car Club of America events. A team of TR2s also did well in the Mille Miglia and the 24 Hours of Le Mans. The car was the least expensive model capable of over 100 mph (160 km/h). For style and sheer chutzpah, it matched the very best.

FIRST MANUFACTURED:
1953 (until 1955)
ENGINE:
1,991 cc Straight Four
PERFORMANCE:
Tests by *Motor* magazine gave a top speed of 107.3 mph (172.8 km/h), and 0-60 mph (97 km/h) in 12.0 secs.
YOU SHOULD KNOW:
You may come across a car called a 'long door' Triumph TR2. These were the 1953 and early 1954 line production models, with doors that extended to the very edge of the car. A shorter door style was introduced in the autumn of 1954, which appears on the majority of TR2s.

Vauxhall PA Cresta

Few cars are so evocative of Britain's late '50s' obsession with American culture as the PA range. The introduction of the PA Cresta was the culmination of several years' gradual Americanization of the Vauxhall marque and the drift away from the small-car market with which it had been associated in the pre-war years. General Motors (Vauxhall's parent company) had given the first subtle signs that the marque was evolving in a new direction with the introduction of the Wyvern family saloon in 1948, and by 1954 understated echoes of American styling had become apparent in Vauxhall's Velox and Cresta saloon range, indicating the start of a new era in design that paved the way for the 1957 launch of the PA Cresta, a deluxe version of the PA Velox.

The PA's flashy tailfins, clustered rear lights, whitewall tyres and wrap-around windows were blatantly transatlantic, emulating the brash good looks of the Buicks and Cadillacs rolling off General Motors' Detroit assembly line. Its paintwork came in bright (optional two-tone) colours with plenty of gleaming chrome trim while the plush interior was fitted with leather upholstery and pile carpet, and included the luxury of a fitted heater as standard. Three people could easily sit together along the front benchseat, with the handbrake neatly stowed under the dashboard and the gearshift mounted on the steering column, leaving the floor completely clear for feet. A beautifully designed tri-sectioned rear screen gave panoramic visibility while the all-sync three-speed gearbox and independent front suspension ensured a smooth ride.

If the starchier members of the establishment considered the PA too *outré* for words, it was certainly the prestige statement car that every hip '50s' glamour-seeker aspired to. More than 81,000 PA Crestas were built and today it is a highly sought-after classic.

FIRST MANUFACTURED:
1957 (until 1962)
ENGINE:
2,262 cc Straight Six ('pushrod' OHV until 1960)
PERFORMANCE:
Top speed of 90 mph (144 km/h) with acceleration of 0-60 mph (97 km/h) in 16.8 secs
YOU SHOULD KNOW:
Ironically, despite (or maybe because of) the PA Cresta's rock 'n' roll image, the Queen of England had a rare estate version for her own personal use.

The semi-transatlantic Cresta appeared when General Motors decided that Britain was ready to embrace rock 'n' roll styling.

1960s

AC Shelby Cobra

One of the top 1960s' sports cars, renowned for both speed and looks, the Cobra is a winning combination of lightweight British roadster and hefty high-torque American Ford V8 engine. Whether you regard it as a British or an American car depends entirely on which side of the Atlantic your loyalty lies. Texan racing star Carroll Shelby certainly considered it his baby – he even declared that the name 'Cobra' had come to him in a dream, and after AC went bankrupt in 1967 he sued for rights and won acknowledgement that he was the maker of every Cobra in the USA, even though they had indisputably been designed and partly built in AC's Thames Ditton workshop.

The Cobra story starts in 1961. Shelby expressed interest in fitting a V8 engine into AC's Ace competition roadster, which had hitherto been equipped with a straight six. A prototype was produced and the Cobra was born. The first 75 were fitted with a Ford 260 HiPo 4.2 litre engine while another 51 had the larger 289 (4.7 litre). At the end of 1962, Alan Turner, AC's chief engineer, made major modifications and fitted new steering using a VW Beetle column. About 530 of these Mark II versions were produced but they were outperformed on the race track and in 1965 the Mark III was designed to be powered by a whopping 'side-oiler' Ford 427 7 litre engine. AC sent some 300 rolling chassis to Shelby and at the same time produced a narrow-fendered AC 289 version for the European market.

The Cobra was almost too fast for its own good. Legend has it that racing driver Jack Sears reached 185 mph (298 km/h) on the M1 in 1964, supposedly a contributory factor to the government's decision to introduce speed limits on British roads.

FIRST MANUFACTURED:
1961 (until1967)
ENGINE:
4.2 l (260 cid); 4.7 l (289 cid);
7 l (427 cid) V8
PERFORMANCE:
Top speed of around 163 mph
(262 km/h) in standard model and 180
mph (290 km/h) in competition model;
0-60 mph (97 km/h)
in 4.2 secs
YOU SHOULD KNOW:
In 2006, Carroll Shelby's own Cobra
sold at auction in Arizona for a record
$5.5 million.

The AC Shelby Cobra was often copied, but never bettered.

Alvis TF21

Alvis had a 'good' World War II, switching from the specialist car market to the manufacture of aero engines thus ensuring a healthy profit. But the war had shaken up society, creating a more egalitarian climate in which the minority privilege of elite sports cars and luxury tourers had no place. This top-end specialist market had been Alvis's customer base so it isn't surprising that the company folded; the only wonder is how it was able to give such a long-lasting swansong.

Alvis's final cars were an imaginative line of 3 litre saloons and drophead coupes, starting with the TA21 in 1950 and ending with the TF21 in 1966 – the last-ever Alvis car. Alvis's short-stroke six-cylinder 3 litre engine supplied plenty of power whatever the revs (150 bhp in the TF21) but carriagework was a dying art and Alvis were only able to go into production by going abroad – to renowned Swiss coachbuilder Hermann Graber. Together with Mulliner Park Ward, by now a subsidiary of Rolls Royce, Graber saved the day. He built some stupendous one-off models while Mulliner produced the rest in batches to his modified design.

The TF21 was the model with which the company closed its doors on the car industry for good, with not a whimper but, rather, a thundering great bang. Though it is generally agreed that the apotheosis of the 3 litre series was a remarkably beautiful Graber-inspired TD21, there is something incredibly special about the TF21. Only 106 were ever made and the experience of sitting behind the wheel of this luxurious motor easily beats driving a contemporaneous Jaguar or Bentley. Alvis faded from the car market with its reputation still at its height. Sadly the company was swallowed up by British Leyland in 1967 and reverted to general engineering.

The TF21 was the last in a long and illustrious line of fine gentleman's sports tourers with a 'Made in Britain' label.

FIRST MANUFACTURED:
1966
ENGINE:
2,993 cc Straight Six
PERFORMANCE:
Top speed of 120 mph (193 km/h)
YOU SHOULD KNOW:
Founded in Coventry by engineer T G John (1880–1946) originally a naval architect, Alvis made exclusive cars for 47 years (1920–1967) which are renowned for their character and the high quality of their workmanship. They have survived well and are still driven in competition racing. A TF21 drophead coupe in good condition can cost around $65,000.

Aston Martin DB5

Possibly the most successful example ever of car product placement, the DB5 achieved film star status in its own right in the hands of Sean Connery as James Bond's over-the-top set of wheels in the film *Goldfinger*. The must-haves for the car chase in the hills above Monte Carlo included twin pop-out 30 calibre Browning machine guns, a three-way revolving front number plate, smokescreen generator, spiked nail dispenser, oil-slick spray nozzle to dispatch tailgaters and a passenger-seat ejector for the instant removal of unwanted company. The car's starring role in the film led to sales of over a thousand DB5s – a record for the Aston Martin company. The DB5 was the epitome of style and if your sights were trained on Miss Moneypenny, the DB5 was the unchallenged transport of delight.

The DB5 replaced the relatively long-lasting DB4, in two-door, four-seater coupe, convertible or estate versions. The DB4's 3.7 litre engine was revved up to 4 litres for the DB5. Earlier models

Unluckily for drivers of the standard DB5, it lacked the James Bond machine guns that would have made the onset of road rage seriously interesting.

maintained the DB4's four-speed manual transmission plus optional overdrive, or the three-speed automatic alternative but these systems were soon superseded by a standard five-speed manual gearbox. The three SU carburettors of the earlier DB5 model produced a top speed of about 140 mph (225 km/h). The Aston Martin Volante, introduced in late 1964, was slightly more powerful.

While its price/performance ratio couldn't match such contemporaries as the Jaguar E-Type (at about half the price tag), the DB5's classic design was infinitely more refined than the E-Type's blatantly vulgar appearance. With its leather upholstery and classy wood interior fittings (though without power steering), it was a machine for the financially inoculated to die for, or even use as their licence for thrills.

FIRST MANUFACTURED:
1963 (until 1965)
ENGINE:
3,995 cc Straight Six
PERFORMANCE:
Top speed of 140 mph (225 km/h);
0-60 mph (97 km/h) in 8.1 secs
YOU SHOULD KNOW:
The Aston Martin DB series was named after David Brown, its managing director. He bought the company in 1947 and sold it in 1972.

Daimler DS420

FIRST MANUFACTURED:
1968 (until 1992)
ENGINE:
4,235 cc V8
PERFORMANCE:
Top speed of 110 mph (177 km/h);
0-60 mph (97 km/h) in 10.5 secs
YOU SHOULD KNOW:
Jaguar supremo John Egan obviously
had faith in his own products – it is
said that in the mid-1980s his DS420
was a mobile boardroom fitted with
a TV, computer with printer and the
inevitable drinks cabinet.

The venerable Daimler company had gone as an independent entity but the new owner – Jaguar– let the name live on. In 1968 the last 'real' Daimler – the stately DR450 limousine – was replaced by the Daimler DS420. An unmistakable Daimler fluted grille remained, but the front end was given Jaguar four-headlight treatment and the new limo was built on a stretched Jaguar 420G floorpan at the Vanden Plas works. It also had a 4.2 litre straight six Jaguar engine.

However, the DS420's aspirations were altogether more upmarket. For this was Jaguar's cheeky attempt to take on the Rolls-Royce Phantom VI – a contest that wasn't entirely one-sided. The two luxury limousines were the same size with automatic transmission, independent suspension and disc brakes all round ensuring that the Daimler's ride was smooth and safe. Better still, it was half the Roller's price.

Various trim levels were available – from luxurious to opulent – and the DS420 had a glass screen allowing back-seat passengers to ride in splendid isolation from the chauffeur – suggesting the target market consisted of up-and-coming company directors who liked to travel in style. It was also popular at senior government level (home and abroad) and used by top hotels to pamper premium guests. Last but not least it was much used in the matched-and-dispatched trade, sweeping brides to church (in white) or transporting grieving relatives and, suitably modified, the dear departed to funerals (in black).

This stately limousine really was a child of the Sixties, albeit a decidedly well-bred one.

Over the years around 4,100 DS420s were built, suggesting that Jaguar's ambitious plan was not without commercial merit. Production transferred to the company's Coventry plant in 1979, but the only change came in the shape of larger bumpers and a new rear numberplate surround. The enduring quality of these hand-built beauties is such that most are still around to delight dedicated drivers of a distinguished modern classic.

Ford Cortina Mk I

As the Swinging Sixties got into gear, Ford was smarting from the mauling it was receiving from the trendy car of the moment – BMC's iconic Mini. Ford couldn't afford to retool to produce a competitive small car, so the company went with what it knew best – a new family saloon. The Cortina Mk I duly appeared in 1962 to take on Vauxhall Victors and Morris Oxfords.

Initially this angular car with tapering flutes along the sides and signature 'Y' rear light clusters was the Consul Cortina, but a cosmetic facelift in 1964 saw the Consul bit quietly buried. The Cortina had arrived, and would be around for some time. It came with two or four doors, there was a choice of engines (1.2 litre or 1.5 litre) and trim levels (standard and deluxe).

It wasn't long before the Cortina family started reproducing. The 1500 Super arrived in January 1963, identified by tapered chrome strips along the flutes. A GT model with twin carbs, front disc brakes and modified suspension followed a month later. An estate car in deluxe or super made its debut in March, with the latter sporting fake wood panelling on the sides and tailgate. Over a million Mk Is would be sold, laying the foundations for what followed.

The Cortina just went from strength to strength. A Mk II version appeared in 1967, followed by the Mk III in 1970. The Mk IV occupied the 1975–1979 slot and the Cortina 80 was the last of the line, the very final one being a silver Crusader that rolled off the Dagenham line in the summer of 1982. It had been a more-than-modest success along the way, becoming the UK's bestseller from 1967 until 1981, with 4.35 million units sold during the extended production run.

FIRST MANUFACTURED:
1962 (until 1966)
ENGINE:
1,198 cc or 1,498 cc Straight Four
PERFORMANCE:
With 1.5 l engine – top speed of 85 mph (138 km/h); 0-60 mph (97 km/h) in 21 secs
YOU SHOULD KNOW:
The Cortina's name was derived from the glamorous Italian ski resort of Cortina d'Ampezzo in the Italian Dolomites (which was cheeky, as Triumph had first used the Dolomite name in 1934) – and a notorious Ford publicity stunt saw Cortinas driven down the resort's fearsome bobsled run.

Its Y-shaped rear lamp cluster was the Cortina's signature.

Ford Lotus Cortina

Although it was technically a variation on the Ford Cortina Mk I theme, the brilliant Ford Lotus Cortina deserves an entry all its own. This was one of the most interesting British saloon cars of the 1960s, making its debut in 1963 as the result of a partnership between Ford and Lotus Cars.

Lotus supremo Colin Chapman had developed a twin-cam version of the Ford Kent engine for racing purposes. Ford's competition department asked Chapman to fit this into a thousand Ford saloons, so they could rally and race in Group 2. The deal was swiftly done and the Type 28 was born. Ford called it the Cortina Lotus, but for once the

little guy won out and the world remembers this splendid custom car as the Lotus Cortina – which undoubtedly had a better ring to the target market of boy racers. Lotus did the mechanical stuff while Ford handled distribution and marketing.

A reinforced two-door Cortina shell provided innocent-looking wrapping around a potent 1.6 litre twin-cam Lotus engine that belted out 105 bhp. Lowered and revised suspension plus servo-assisted disc brakes ensured that the Lotus Cortina handled well, with wide road wheels and tyres providing limpet-like grip. Nobody who tried to beat one of these stylish sprinters away from the traffic lights had any doubts about what they'd just run up against – but just in case someone thought this special sports saloon was any old Cortina, a white paint job and green side flash proclaimed the Lotus Cortina's exclusive parentage.

Ford wanted to continue with the cooperative venture when the Mk II Cortina appeared, but Lotus declined and the Lotus Cortina Mk II was produced entirely by Ford from 1966 until 1970, with the Lotus badge being replaced by a bland 'Twin Cam' announcement after a few months.

FIRST MANUFACTURED:
1963 (until 1966)
ENGINE:
1,558 cc DOHC Straight Four
PERFORMANCE:
Top speed of 108 mph (174 km/h);
0-60 mph (97 km/h) in 10.1 secs
YOU SHOULD KNOW:
The aim of creating a great sports racer was successful, with the Lotus Cortina enjoying many race victories. Unfortunately, it was prone to mechanical problems when used as a road car, but was so exciting that besotted owners easily forgave its faults.

Naughty, naughty – the Lotus Cortina was really a powerful street-legal racing car.

The GT40 dominated the Le Mans 24 race in the late Sixties.

Ford GT40

Every competitive carmaker in the 1960s wanted to poke the all-conquering Maranello boys in the eye. Ford was no exception, fuelled by Enzo Ferrari's abrupt termination of negotiations to sell his company to Ford. Whilst the decision to go head-to-head with Ferrari came from slighted Henry Ford II in America, design-and-build work took place in Britain.

The sensational result was the Ford GT (later named the GT40). Ford's attack on the international endurance race circuit was not entirely motivated by pique – for sustained track success was the best advertising money couldn't buy. The development team included Eric Broadley, owner-designer of the advanced Lola GT mid-engined racecar, and a new factory was established at Slough. The prototype was unveiled in April 1964.

This was powered by a 4.2 litre Ford Fairlane engine and – though not a winner – put in track time that helped finalize the Mk I's design. This had a 4.7 litre engine and 50 were built to satisfy production sports car regulations. But it still wasn't a winner, so the Mk II saw the introduction of a monstrous 7 litre engine that had been tried and tested on American racetracks, together with bodywork tweaks to accommodate it.

Ford had cracked it – the GT40 Mk II secured a 1-2-3 finish at Daytona. In 1966 there was a prestigious 1-2-3 in the Le Mans 24 ahead of Ferrari and Henry Ford II's mission was accomplished. Meanwhile, a Mk III was built for road use, fitted with a 4.7 litre engine, but this wasn't a success (seven produced). Still, Le Mans fell to a GT40 Mk IV in 1967 and two more Le Mans wins would follow in 1968 and 1969. And there, sadly, the extraordinary GT40 story effectively ended – its successor was the evolutionary G7A, built and campaigned in America.

FIRST MANUFACTURED:
1965 (until 1968)
ENGINE:
4.2 l (256 cid), 4.7 l (288.5 cid)
or 7.0 l (427 cid) V8
PERFORMANCE:
Mk III road car – top speed of
160 mph (257 km/h); 0-60 mph
(97 km/h) in 5.3 secs
YOU SHOULD KNOW:
Ford's attempt to stage a dead-heat at the end of the 1966 Le Mans 24 race came unstuck when, despite the neck-and-neck finish, Bruce McClaren and Chris Amon were declared the winners, having started further back down the track than second-placed Ken Miles – who was thus denied a heroic hat trick of GT40 wins at Sebring, Daytona and Le Mans in the same year.

Ford Escort Mk I

Although used to identify an estate car version of the Ford Anglia 100E, and appearing on various Ford cars sold in North America, the Escort name started writing a long chapter in the history of European motoring with the debut of the Ford Escort Mk I in late 1967. The long-running Ford Anglia's replacement had to be fit for mass-market purpose, and was.

First up was a two-door saloon with a curving waistline and characteristic 'dog-bone' front grille with headlamps at either end. A three-door estate appeared in spring 1968 and a tradesman's van followed a year later. The four-door saloon did not arrive until 1969. There was the usual Ford options package – different trim levels (De Luxe and Super) and a choice of engines (1.1 litre or 1.3 litre). It wasn't long before a specialist performance version appeared in the form of a 1300GT with tuned engine and Weber carburettor. A further variation with the same engine set-up was the Sport, with flared front wings, which in turn spawned the 1300E with fancy executive touches like a wood-trimmed dashboard.

Ford was a great believer in the power of race wins when it came to selling road cars and the Escort Twin Cam was a high-performance competition model fitted with a 1.6 litre engine tweaked by Lotus Cars and assembled at Ford's AVO (Advanced Vehicle Operation) facility at Aveley. The investment was shrewd, with Escort Mk Is sweeping all before them on the rally circuit and going on to become one of the most successful rally cars of all time.

That contributed to the Escort's massive commercial success, especially in Britain where it comfortably outsold its General Motors competitor, the Vauxhall Viva – though to be fair GM hit back in Europe where the Opel Kadett won out.

FIRST MANUFACTURED:
1967 (until 1974)
ENGINE:
940 cc (rarely), 1,098 cc, 1,298 cc and 1,558 cc Straight Four
PERFORMANCE:
1300 Sport – top speed of 98 mph (158 km/h)
YOU SHOULD KNOW:
The Escort Mk I's reach was long – it was not only built at Halewood and Saarlouis in Germany, but also assembled in Australia and New Zealand.

The Escort had a massive commercial success in Britain with soaring sales.

The Escort had something to offer everyone, from working man to racing driver.

What's good for America is worth trying in Europe, thought Ford, and were duly rewarded when their Capri pony car hit the spot.

Ford Capri Mk 1

The European idea of a perfect pony car (long front, short back) was the Ford Capri – or more accurately it was Ford Europe's idea. The recently created conglomerate launched this trendy car in 1969, hoping to emulate the Mustang's success in North America. The Capri was based on the Cortina platform and had common styling but different engine specs for Britain and the Continent.

Ford wanted to produce a fashionable car that would appeal to the widest possible market (or, to put it another way, every pocket). Thus a variety of engines was offered. The initial UK options were 1.3 litre or 1.6 litre versions of the Ford Kent straight four, with a 2 litre Cologne V6 topping the offering. Before long, Brits with lots of dosh could choose sports versions like the 3000 GT with the Ford Essex V6 engine. That's the one that always featured in memorable car chases in 1970s' TV series like *The Professionals*, frequently ending in a slewing handbrake emergency stop followed by a bonnet roll and brisk gunplay.

Competition glory was never far from Ford's mind, and a souped-up Capri duly appeared in 1971, powered by a 2.6 litre version of the Cologne V6 assembled by Weslake and featuring alloy cylinder heads. This was the Capri RS2600, which would prove to be a star of the European Touring Car Championship in the early 1970s. Never slow to appreciate the powerful aphrodisiac properties of track success, a luxury road-going version with a detuned engine and double-barrel Solex carb was available.

Business was encouragingly brisk, but Ford still gave the Mk 1 a facelift in 1972, introducing better suspension, more comfortable seats, rectangular headlights and enlarged tail lights. A significant revamp saw the larger Capri Mk 2 arrive in February 1974, complete with hatchback rear door.

FIRST MANUFACTURED:
1969 (to 1974)
ENGINE:
1,298 cc or 1,598 cc Straight Four, 2,550 cc or 2,994 cc V6
PERFORMANCE:
3000 GT – top speed of 122 mph (196 km/h); 0-60 mph (97 km/h) in 8.4 secs
YOU SHOULD KNOW:
The original choice of name for the Capri was the Ford Colt – but Mitsubishi had cleverly trademarked that iconic American title so Capri it became, revisiting the not-altogether-different Consul Capri of the early 1960s and borrowing a model name used by various Ford-owned marques in America.

Ginetta G4

Who says there was no room for the start-up automobile entrepreneur in post-war Britain? The four Walklett Brothers certainly managed to found a successful car manufacturing business in 1958 (in the wilds of Suffolk) and ran it until their retirement in 1989.

The Ginetta G4 was an early introduction, in 1961. It had a fibreglass convertible roadster body that sported tailfins and was fitted with a Ford 105E engine. Unlike its immediate predecessors, the G4 was not designed specifically for competition use, though it was successful in that sphere. It was a classic 'drive to the track and race' car, which was equally at home on a motor-racing circuit or strutting its stuff to admiring glances when used as a road car.

This lightweight car had a space-frame chassis with double wishbones, coil springs and dampers in the front. Rear suspension consisted of a Ford live axle and there were drum brakes. Over the years the G4 enjoyed considerable evolution and improvement. A selection of Ford engines was offered, including a 1.3 litre Classic, 1.6 litre X-flow and a 1.5 litre Cortina GT power plant.

With the introduction of Series II in 1963, the roadster was joined by a coupe, which was essentially the same car with an add-on hardtop. At the same time a BMC rear axle replaced the Ford live axle. The tailfins were dropped and enhancements such as disc brakes were introduced to improve all-round handling and performance. The G4 Series III took over in 1966, though the only obvious change was then-modish pop-up headlights that rested on the front bumper when not in use.

Around 500 of these zippy sports racers were built in the 1960s and they still compete regularly at classic meets, piloted by enthusiastic drivers who appreciate unmistakably British motoring heritage.

FIRST MANUFACTURED:
1961 (until 1969)
ENGINE:
Various, but originally a 997 cc
Straight Four
PERFORMANCE:
1 litre engine – top speed of
105 mph (169 km/h)
YOU SHOULD KNOW:
This great British sports car rides again
in the form of the contemporary DARE
Ginetta G4 – a sleek sports racer with
a 1.8 litre Ford Zetec that delivers a top
speed of 130 mph (209 km/h) and a
0-60 mph (97 km/h) time of 5.8 secs.

The G4 offered the evolutionary choice of many Ford engines during its production run.

Hillman Imp

FIRST MANUFACTURED:
1963 (until 1976)
ENGINE:
874 cc Straight Four
PERFORMANCE:
Top speed of 80 mph (129 km/h);
0-50 mph (80 km/h) in 14.7 secs
YOU SHOULD KNOW:
Rootes produced some special Imp
derivatives like the Imp Californian, and
nifty badge engineering transformed
the Basic Imp into desirable
alternatives like the Singer Chamois,
the Sunbeam Stiletto and Sunbeam
Sport with its tuned
twin-carb engine.

BMC's Mini caused a sensation in 1959, and rival manufacturers were caught on the hop by the popularity of that innovative new small car. But they all wanted a piece of the action and the Rootes Group's belated response was the Hillman Imp, which appeared in 1963.

It was a huge gamble. Rootes had little experience of small-car production and the Imp (codenamed 'Apex') required a new factory, as further development at the company's Ryton base was impossible. The chosen site (after government arm-twisting and provision of generous grants) was Linwood near Glasgow. This necessitated a long round-trip for Linwood parts finished at Ryton, and involved a militant Scottish workforce prone to striking first and talking later. An added difficulty was the fact that the Imp's aluminium engine was another leap into the unknown.

All that considered, the Imp turned out to be an interesting and popular car. There were teething troubles after the daring design was rushed into production, but despite that the distinctive Imp was well received, being cheap to buy and economical to run. A lightweight engine was mounted behind the rear wheels and this required sophisticated rear suspension to counteract an inevitable tendency to oversteer.

The original Imp was a two-door saloon with a rear hatch. A coupe version was added in 1965. That year also saw the introduction of a van and estate car (effectively a van with windows), though these were discontinued in 1970. The Imp got a major revamp in 1966 to iron out early mechanical problems and Rootes continued to improve this attractive little car throughout its life. Around 440,000 were built, and they're as much fun to drive today as they were then. But ultimately the Rootes gamble failed – the expensive Linwood venture eventually ruined the company.

Rootes' chirpy rival to BMC's Mini was troubled by logistics and strikes but still sold well.

Jaguar E-Type

The E-Type was a genuine world beater – enough said?

The golden era of Jaguar Cars got off to a great start with the XK120 and XK150, but the company really hit the jackpot with the E-Type (XK-E in America). This is regarded as the finest-looking sports car of all time ('The most beautiful car ever made' was Enzo Ferrari's verdict) and also the most influential – leading the way for many fabulous brethren that made the 1960s a seminal decade for super sports cars.

Series 1 was launched in 1961, consisting of two-door convertibles and coupes with a 3.8 litre engine carried over from the XK150S. The cars featured torsion bar front ends with independent rear suspension and disc brakes all round. A 4.2 litre engine was introduced in 1964, along with styling changes. The 2+2 version with a stretched coupe body appeared in 1966 and further modifications followed to meet American requirements, sufficient to justify the Series 1.5 tag applied by some.

Series 2 followed in 1968, retaining the 4.2 litre engine and all three body styles. Modifications towards the end of Series 1 were extended to meet US regulations, which also required the triple-carb UK engine to be detuned. Headlights had lost glass covers, a wraparound rear bumper appeared and the cooling system was improved. New seats added comfort, whilst air conditioning and power steering were optional extras. Series 2 carried the E-Type forward into the 1970s.

Series 3 ran from 1971 to 1975, and saw the introduction of a 5.3 litre V12, discontinuation of the short-wheelbase coupe and switch of the convertible to the longer 2+2 floorpan. The cars acquired an aggressive slatted grille, flared wheel arches . . . and boastful V12 badge. With 15,000 Series 3s completing an overall production run of 70,000, it was a fitting climax to 15 years of breathtaking sporting motoring.

FIRST MANUFACTURED:
1961 (until 1975)
ENGINE:
3,781 cc, 4,235 cc Straight Six;
5,344 cc V12
PERFORMANCE:
Series 1 with 3.8 litre engine – top
speed of 149 mph (238 km/h);
0-60 mph (97 km/h) in 7.1 secs
YOU SHOULD KNOW:
The rarest E-Types are either those
from the first batch of 500, which have
flat floors and external bonnet catches
(after which the floors were swiftly
modified to provide more leg room
and bonnet catches were repositioned
internally) or the few Series 3 cars built
using the old
4.2 litre straight six engine.
Take your pick!

The E-Type made a great impression even on Enzo Ferrari who declared it 'the most beautiful car ever made'.

Jaguar Mk X

FIRST MANUFACTURED:
1961 (until 1965)
ENGINE:
3,718 cc or 4,235 cc Straight Six
PERFORMANCE:
With 4.2 litre engine – top speed of 123
mph (198 km/h); 0-60 mph
(97 km/h) in 10.4 secs
YOU SHOULD KNOW:
After all that effort put into producing
a BIG car pitched at the American
market, it did not sell well in the
States. Just a small percentage of
the 19,000 Mk X/420Gs built actually
crossed the Atlantic.

This top-of-the-range luxury car was completely different from its Mk IX predecessor and a bit of a monster by European standards – fully six feet (two metres) wide. That was because it was principally designed for the United States market where big was beautiful and petrol consumption immaterial.

Jaguar's big saloon had independent suspension and a 3.7 litre engine, which was replaced by a 4.2 litre plant in 1964. Triple carburettors helped to deliver performance comparable with American V8 engines twice the size, and for all its bulk the Mk X was a speedy car when pedal hit metal. Perhaps that isn't too surprising, as the engine was borrowed from the E-Type Jag. Power steering was standard, which ensured that this gargantuan car wasn't hard to handle.

The Mk X was the first car to have the signature Jaguar face of four headlights set into rounded wings, and the sumptuous old-fashioned interior was notable by the ultimate wood finish. There was timber everywhere – dashboard, around windows, housing various controls – and even the handy tables that folded down behind the front seats were stoutly constructed of matching wood.

Technically, production of the Mk X ended in 1965 with the introduction of the Jaguar 420G (not to be confused with the 420 compact sporting saloon produced between 1966 and 1968, which was virtually the same as the Daimler Sovereign). But in fact this was merely a name change and the rebadged 420G was effectively a Mk X Series 2. There were cosmetic design changes and a stretched version was offered to permit the installation of a glass screen – and the floorpan was lengthened further when the Daimler DS 420 was launched in 1968, with the two luxury limousines effectively being badge-engineered non-identical twins.

The Jaguar Mk X was big, but sadly not very beautiful.

Jaguar XJ Mk 1 Series 1

Jaguar's strenuous efforts to make the grade as an upmarket volume purveyor of quality saloon cars took a step forward in 1968 with the introduction of the all-new XJ Series 1. The launch of the XJ (from Xperimental Jaguar) Series consolidated the company's saloon car offering into a single range. New XJ models provided a superb replacement for existing Jaguars (S-Type Mk 2, 420 and 420G, plus their Daimler counterparts) and the line would continue to be produced into the 1990s.

First out of the box was the XJ6 Mk 1. These comfortable saloons came with a choice of two straight sixes – 2.8 litre and 4.2 litre versions of Jaguar's renowned twin-cam XK engine. The former was considered to be somewhat underpowered and the latter outsold it by three to one. Power steering was standard and there was a choice of manual or automatic transmission. With either engine the XJ6 was famous for silky-smooth performance and crisp handling.

The particularly graceful styling was classic 'four-headlamp' Jaguar and the interior was lavishly appointed with wood and leather upholstery in the marque's finest traditions. A long-wheelbase version of the 4.2 litre XJ6 appeared towards the end of the run, offering more rear legroom, as did the top-of-the-range XJ12 with its powerful 5.3 litre V12 engine.

Around 82,000 Series 1 XJs were produced, plus another 16,000 of the Daimler equivalents of each Jaguar type, so there are still plenty around for anyone who owns a petrol station to drive and enjoy. Series 2 appeared in 1973 and did not acquire the best of reputations, with allegations of shoddy build quality said to stem from Jaguar's absorption into the British Leyland Group. The cars themselves weren't so different from Series 1 examples, but were modified to meet US regulations.

FIRST MANUFACTURED:
1968 (until 1973)
ENGINE:
2,790 cc or 4,235 cc Straight Six; 5,343 cc V12
PERFORMANCE:
With 2.6 litre engine – top speed of 118 mph (190 km/h); 0-60 mph (97 km/h) in 10.5 secs
YOU SHOULD KNOW:
During the initial launch campaign Jaguar boss Sir William Lyons described the XJ6 as 'the finest Jaguar ever' – but he would say that, wouldn't he? Actually, he knew a little something – Series 1 cars are universally considered to have the best build quality and are definitely the most collectable XJs.

The Series 1 Jaguar XJs were sleek and fast, a combination that brought commercial success.

According to Jaguar boss Sir William Lyons, the XJ6 was 'the finest Jaguar ever'.

Jensen Interceptor and Jensen FF

Jensen Motors was founded by brothers Richard and Alan, who made vehicle bodies before World War II and were soon producing their own cars. The first Interceptor appeared in 1949 – a coupe with an Austin Six engine and a pioneering fibreglass body. The Jensen 541 replaced it in 1953, despite the demands of a major contract to produce bodies for the Austin-Healey sports cars. In 1961, production of bodies for Volvo's P1800 was added and the booming company introduced the Jensen CV-8.

But the CV-8 soon looked dated, and Jensen decided to compete with big boys like Aston Martin and those luscious Latins. Although the CV-8's updated chassis, Chrysler V8 engine and TorqueFlite automatic transmission were up to the job, Italian styling was called for. A design by Carrozzeria Touring was realized by Vignale, who created the first production bodies. This stunning new fastback bore the revived Interceptor name and its look was distinctive, with a squarish front and rounded rear topped by a huge curved rear window that was also a hinged hatchback. The interior with its wood and leather was, however, reassuringly British.

Despite intense competition in the luxury GT market, the Interceptor sold well throughout the '60s and into the mid-1970s, despite build-quality problems and serious commercial pressures created by the collapse of Jensen's core body-building business. The

The Interceptor not only looked stunning, but also delivered a superb level of performance.

Mk II arrived in 1969 and the Mk III in 1971 with a bigger engine. A yummy convertible was introduced in 1974 and a coupe in 1975.

The stylish Interceptor is deserving of a more-than-honourable mention in the book of British automotive success stories, but in many respects its importance is outweighed by that of a commercially unsuccessful companion model. Jensen Motors had been working with Harry Ferguson (of Massey-Ferguson tractor fame) since the early 1960s, and the innovative Irish engineer was intent on producing an effective four-wheel-drive system for race and road cars.

In 1961 the Ferguson P99 Climax scored a notable first and last. In the hands of Stirling Moss it became the first four-wheel-drive car – and last front-engined car – to win a Formula 1 race. On the road front, the joint venture led to the Jensen CV-8 FF shown at the Earls Court Motor Show in 1965. This was the debut of the FF road-car system (FF stood for Ferguson Formula) and it anticipated the world's first four-wheel drive supercar.

This was the Jensen FF, which deployed Ferguson's four-wheel drive system to great effect, also offering Dunlop Maxaret anti-lock braking, traction control and power steering. It shared Chrysler TorqueFlite transmission and 6.3 litre V8 motor with the Interceptor. To all intents and purposes the two models were identical, though in fact the FF had a slightly longer wheelbase and an extra cooling vent in the front bumper. But technically it was a world ahead and was better to drive than the Interceptor, adding leech-like roadholding to its sibling's many qualities.

Unfortunately, mechanical complexity made it difficult – and expensive – to produce. Jensen FFs were built to order only, and the steep price ensured that relatively few were sold – some 320 in six years. And when Jensen started struggling in the early 1970s, the innovative FF was reluctantly discontinued – a classic example of a great car that was ahead of its time.

An attempt to enter the sports car market with the Jensen Healey was made after Donald Healey joined the company in the early '70s, but none of these moves could revive Jensen's fortunes and the company was dissolved in 1976, leaving the splendid Interceptor as a lasting memorial.

This massive rear hatch window was a characteristic design feature of the Interceptor.

FIRST MANUFACTURED:
1966 (until 1971)
ENGINE:
6,286 cc V8
PERFORMANCE:
Top speed of 130 mph (210 km/h);
0-60 mph (97 km/h) in 7.7 secs
YOU SHOULD KNOW:
A drawback that inhibited the Jensen FF's commercial viability was a serious design fault – because of the transmission set-up and steering geometry it couldn't be converted to left-hand drive for the important American luxury GT market. Oops!

Lagonda Rapide

In 1947 entrepreneur David Brown answered a small ad in *The Times* offering a 'High-class motor business for sale' . . . and bought Aston Martin. His spending spree didn't stop, for he also acquired Lagonda . . . which cost more than twice as much as Aston Martin. In fact, the bargain buy would be the winner and Lagonda an also-ran.

At first everything went well. The first post-war Lagonda engine – designed by the legendary W O Bentley – not only appeared in the handsome Lagonda 2.6 litre drophead coupe of 1948 but would also power the great Aston Martins of the 1950s. The 2.6 was succeeded by the 3 litre coupe (fixed or drophead) and saloon in 1953, but when that was discontinued in 1958 and not replaced it was generally assumed the Lagonda marque was toast.

But no! David Brown may have been busy winning races with his Astons, but he found time to develop another Lagonda – the elegant Rapide, styled by Touring in Milan, launched in 1961 and based on the Aston Martin DB4. This long, low saloon was every bit as elegant as its predecessors. It had a 4 litre engine, lightweight chassis and aluminium body. There were servo-assisted disc brakes all round and an automatic four-speed gearbox. The interior featured a mandatory burr walnut dashboard and leather upholstery. It lived up to its name with an impressive top speed as David Brown tried to resurrect the four-door performance GT format.

He was delighted with the result, but sadly cash-rich buyers were slow to appreciate the opportunity they were missing. The Rapide was built to order, and only 55 of those were taken in four years. The last Lagonda was hand-built in 1964 and if you don't already own one, don't bother to go looking.

FIRST MANUFACTURED:
1961 (until 1964)
ENGINE:
3,995 cc Straight Six
PERFORMANCE:
Top speed of 130 mph; 0-60 mph (97 km/h) in 10.2 secs
YOU SHOULD KNOW:
The combined price David Brown paid for both Aston Martin and Lagonda in 1947 was less than £75,000 – which in turn was only half the average price of ONE Aston Martin Lagonda, the stunning supercar launched thirty years later.

Lotus Elan

The Lotus Elan roadster was a welcome debutant in 1962 – welcome to the manufacturer because it replaced the expensive-to-build Elite and welcomed by sporting drivers who appreciated performance-packed possibilities. It was even embraced by those who weren't minted but could wield a mean spanner, as the Elan was initially offered in kit form like the successful Lotus Seven.

The Elan was an uncompromising manifestation of Colin Chapman's lightweight design philosophy and delivered acceleration and top speed far ahead of its time for this class of sports car. The power came from a 1.6 litre evolution version of the sturdy Ford Kent engine that had been fitted with a Lotus-designed Cosworth twin-cam alloy head (the engine also used in the punchy Lotus Cortina). The Elan boasted independent suspension and disc brakes all round long before these became standard features. It had a steel chassis and fibreglass body that kept the weight right down.

With its streamlined shape and pop-up headlamps, this modern-looking roadster was an instant hit. The Elan's favourable reception was complemented by the swift appearance of a hardtop option in 1963 and a two-seater coupe in 1965. The Elan's commercial success was finally cemented by the arrival of the handsome long-wheelbase Elan Plus Two in 1967. This was a genuine 2+2 coupe with a roomy cabin, which retained all the speed and agility of its predecessors – in fact it was even a tad faster, thanks to a slippery aerodynamic shape. The Plus Two continued in production until 1975, two years after the roadster and coupe were discontinued.

The Lotus Elan would be born again in the late 1980s for a six-year production run – differentiated from its illustrious ancestry by an M100 tag and lauded as a technical masterpiece in the finest traditions of advanced Lotus engineering.

FIRST MANUFACTURED:
1962 (until 1975)
ENGINE:
1,558 cc Straight Four
PERFORMANCE:
Top speed of 118 mph (190 km/h);
0-60 mph (97 km/h) in 7.6 secs
YOU SHOULD KNOW:
Nobody could ever accuse the Japanese of being copycats, but it is known that Mazda bought, disassembled and closely studied a couple of first generation Lotus Elans – though of course the close resemblance of the subsequent Mazda MX-5 is a complete coincidence.

Initially a kit-car in classic Lotus mode, the Elan soon proved to be a sporty factory-built winner with buyers.

Marcos 1800 GT

The Marcos biography covers a succession of bankruptcies interrupted by interesting cars, starting with the company's foundation in 1959 by Frank Costin and Jem Marsh. Their first effort was a GT that appeared in 1960 with then-fashionable gullwing doors and an odd four-piece windscreen. Nine examples made in the next couple of years had assorted Ford engines teamed with Standard/Triumph steering and suspension. Their most unusual feature was the fact that the chassis was fabricated from laminated plywood – an idea suggested by Costin, who worked on the wood-framed Mosquito fighter bomber in World War II.

After the Adams brothers came aboard they refined the original design and in 1963 the classic 1800 GT coupe was introduced, with hints of E-Type Jaguar in its racy look and long body shape. This was a very pretty car that would continue to be produced for years, through various comings and goings of the Marcos marque. The

Many different engines were offered during the production run of the handsome 1800 GT.

engine was bought in from Volvo and was the same power plant used in the iconic Volvo P1800 of 1961. Later in the 1800 GT's run various different engines were offered as options.

In 1969 the GT effectively became a different car as a steel chassis was introduced, enabling Marcos to fit a range of more powerful engines, including the 3 litre Ford Essex V6 or the similarly sized Volvo straight six. But production ended with the first 'bust' in 1971, when the money ran out as a result of problems getting export clearance for the USA coupled with the crippling development costs of the new Mantis.

Today, surviving Marcos 1800 GTs are prized as classic racing cars, with well-maintained track versions fetching high prices – for they are still great fun to drive and very competitive more than forty years after they first burst onto the scene.

FIRST MANUFACTURED:
1963 (until 1968)
ENGINE:
1,778 cc Straight Four
PERFORMANCE:
Top speed of 116 mph (187 km/h);
0-60 mph (97 km/h) in 8.2 secs
YOU SHOULD KNOW:
The Marcos 1800 GT, named for its engine size, should not be confused with the company's other '1800' – the Mini Marcos of 1965 that had a wheelbase of just 69 inches (1800 mm) and proved to be popular in Japan and quite a little track star in Europe.

MGB

FIRST MANUFACTURED:
1962 (until 1980)
ENGINE:
1,799 cc Straight Four
PERFORMANCE:
Top speed of 103 mph (166 km/h);
0-60 mph (97 km/h) in 12.2 secs
YOU SHOULD KNOW:
For MGB purists, the last year that
really counts is 1973 – for that's
the last year the car was produced
with traditional chrome bumpers,
rather than the large, black rubber
monstrosities introduced the following
year to comply with US regulations.

The rather voluptuous lines of the MGA were starting to look dated as the Swinging Sixties dawned, but the British Motor Corporation was ready with one of its few great success stories – the MGB. This brilliant sports car with its clean lines would be around for nearly twenty years and well over half a million MGBs (and derivatives) would be manufactured, making it the best-selling British sports car of all time.

The two-seater roadster was introduced in 1962, and this neat convertible was joined in 1973 by the hatchback MGB GT coupe – nominally a 2+2, though the rear seating would only have been adequate if Snow White were driving. This version would continue to be produced in virtually unchanged form until it was dropped in 1974, though a meaty V8 evolution was offered from 1973 to 1976.

The roadster had a comfortable interior with wind-up windows and a parcel shelf behind the seats. The car featured a four-cylinder 1.8 litre engine and – unlike the MGA it replaced and the Triumph TRs with which it competed – had monocoque rather than body-on-chassis construction, which reduced weight and costs allowing the MGB to be sold at an attractive price. It was an instant success with sporty drivers because the MGB was (and is) a joy to drive, with good acceleration, excellent roadholding and an ability to top the 'ton' when flat out.

The roadster was upgraded as the Mk II in 1967, with an all-synchromesh gearbox and the option of automatic transmission. Various other cosmetic changes took place until the Mk III was introduced in 1972. This had a better heater and new fascia, and would be the final evolution. The last MGB rolled off the line at Abingdon in 1980, to end the era of mass-produced Great British sports cars.

A classic example of the chrome-bumpered roadster.

EBW 45B

MGC

Mechanically speaking, the MGC's biography is not really so very different from the heart-warming MGB story, for the two models appear to be virtually identical. But that superficial likeness conceals considerable differences. Produced for just three years (1967 to 1969), the MGC was more than a performance-enhanced MGB fitted with a 2.9 litre straight six. It was intended as a replacement for parent company BMC's Austin-Healey 3000, which was discontinued in 1967.

Though both bigger and more powerful than the MGB, the MGC was not a nimble car.

Considerable modification of the MGB platform was required to accommodate the 2.9 litre Morris C-series engine with its polished aluminium head and twin SU carburettors. This took the form of a revised floorpan and bonnet with a characteristic bulge to allow for a raised radiator, plus a neat teardrop for the carburettors. There was a special torsion-bar suspension system with telescopic dampers and the standard gearbox was a four-speed manual. Overdrive or three-speed automatic transmission were options. The wheels were bigger than those on MGBs.

Very much following the MGB formula, both an MGC roadster and MGC GT were offered, but these powerful sports cars never really fired the public imagination. Despite their extra grunt and performance that far exceeded that of the four-cylinder car, the heavy engine adversely affected the nimble handling that had made the MGB so popular. However, the factory did produce a few lightweight MGC GTS racing models, and these competed with some success. The GTS cars were very attractive with flared wings and an aggressive bonnet bulge.

With around 9,000 produced during the shortish production run, the MGC is far rarer than its 'common' relation and therefore much sought-after by MG enthusiasts and collectors of classic sports cars. Happily, modern tyres and a little suspension tweaking can iron out those original handling problems to the complete satisfaction of today's owner-drivers.

FIRST MANUFACTURED:
1967 (until 1969)
ENGINE:
2,912 cc OHV Straight Six
PERFORMANCE:
Top speed of 120 mph (193 km/h);
0-60 mph (97 km/h) in 10 secs
YOU SHOULD KNOW:
Sadly, the MGC would be the last all-new model to be created and produced by this great maker at the company's famous Abingdon works before it was closed in 1980.

Morgan Plus 8

Some people just refuse to move with the times – and thank goodness for that. At least so say the fans (there are many) of the Morgan Motor Company. Founded in 1909, Morgan is based in rural Worcestershire and hand-assembles fine British sports cars that are so coveted that there is inevitably a (sometimes lengthy) list containing the names of those who have put down deposits and can't wait (but must) for their brand-new Morgan to be ready.

Having made a pre-war name with classic three-wheelers, Morgan had launched the company's first 4-4 car (four cylinders, four wheels) in 1936, and it was a derivation of this that appeared as the traditional Morgan Plus 4 sports car in 1950 – a car that would continue to be produced as it evolved steadily into the 21st century.

The next big development was the arrival of the Morgan Plus 8 in 1968 (nothing to do with the number of wheels, but rather the

It certainly looked old-fashioned, but a big engine endowed the Morgan Plus 8 with impressive performance figures.

new Rover V8 engine). Plus 4 and Plus 8 looked similar, but the latter's performance was superior. Indeed, the V8 gave it deceptive oomph, with blistering acceleration and a surprisingly high top speed. To the considerable satisfaction of enthusiasts, Moggies (as Morgans are affectionately known) have never departed from the traditional construction method of steel chassis, ash frame and hand-crafted body – and the resultant lightweight sports car has always offered relatively high performance for an open roadster.

The Plus 8 was continued in production until 2004 (with various engine upgrades along the way), by which time over 3,500 had been produced. They remain collectable British classics that are robust enough to enjoy taking to the road day in, day out (especially in summer with the top down) – and sufficiently rare to ensure that second-hand values remain high.

FIRST MANUFACTURED:
1968 (until 2004)
ENGINE:
3,532 cc V8
PERFORMANCE:
Top speed of 124 mph (200 km/h);
0-60 mph (97 km/h) in 6.7 secs
YOU SHOULD KNOW:
The Plus 8 is fast, but its successor leaves it standing – the retro-styled Aero 8 can scorch from rest to 60 mph in just 4.4 seconds and zip on to a top speed of 170 mph (270 km/h) – not bad for a wooden car!

Peel P50

FIRST MANUFACTURED:
1963 (until 1964)
ENGINE:
49 cc Two Stroke DKW
PERFORMANCE:
Top speed of 38 mph (61 km/h)
YOU SHOULD KNOW:
Fewer than 50 Peel P50s were made, in three choices of colour: red, white or blue. It is estimated that there are only around 20 still in existence, valued at between £35,000 and £50,000. Two original P50s are on the Isle of Man – you can see one in the Peel Transport Museum.

Advertised as being for 'one adult and a shopping bag', the Peel P50 was designed as a convenience microcar for nipping around town. When it was launched at the 1962 Earl's Court Motor Show, it caused a stir on two counts: it was the only car ever to have emanated from the Isle of Man, and it was unlike anything else on the road. The Peel P50 holds the title for smallest-ever production car: a mere 117 cm (46 in) high, 135 cm (53 in) long and 99 cm (39 in) wide, it weighs just 59 kg (130 lb).

This cute little three-wheeler, running on an air-cooled Zweirad Union moped engine, was designed by Cyril Cannell, boss of the Peel Engineering Co. The tubular steel frame and GRP body were largely hand-assembled. It had only one door, one headlight and one windscreen wiper and there was no starter motor – you used a crank lever to get it going – and no speedometer – it was considered unnecessary since you had to go flat out to break the 30 mph speed limit. It had three forward gears and an innovative means of reversing – you just got out and hauled the car backwards by its rear-attached chrome handle. In a 15 mile road test round London the P50 triumphed – reaching the finish 30 minutes before any other car.

The Peel P50 was not a great success: it had poor suspension, tipped over rather too easily and generally felt a bit of a death-trap. However, it was very cheap (under £200) and incredibly economical on fuel. And there was no problem about finding a parking space – you just picked it up and slotted it into any available gap. Ahead of its time, perhaps?

The Peel was great for parking but not recommended when it came to a rear-end shunt.

Reliant Scimitar GTE SE5

Like the Robin, the Scimitar had a fibreglass body, but it actually boasted four wheels.

It all began in 1935 when bicycle company Raleigh decided to discontinue its three-wheeler delivery van. The van's designer was T L Williams, who founded Reliant to take over production. This led to a series of three-wheelers culminating in Reliant Robin economy cars and the extraordinary Bond Bug. However, the company also became active at the opposite end of the performance spectrum. First up was the punchy Reliant Sabre, but this was soon followed by the company's innovative Scimitar.

The Scimitar SE4 appeared in 1964 as a two-door booted coupe. With around a thousand sold, the SE4 was successful enough to encourage the Scimitar's next evolution, which saw the completely redesigned SE5 model introduced late in 1968. With its sturdy chassis and cute fibreglass body, the SE5 was a head turner.

This four-seater GT was based on a design by British consultancy Ogle, which came up with a racy estate car with ample fold-flat rear load space accessed through the hinged, sloping rear window. The only car that came close to a similar layout was the Volvo P1800 estate, but the Reliant True Brit was the preferred repository for the muddy green wellies of sporty country types (famously, the Scimitar would acquire at least one high-profile fan, with the young Princess Anne rarely seen driving anything else).

There was a choice of straight six or V6 engines, but the latter was more powerful and proved the popular choice, leading to the former being dropped. Performance was excellent. The Scimitar had a snappy four-speed manual gearbox that later acquired overdrive, and Borg-Warner automatic transmission was offered as an option. Fewer than 2,500 SE5s were hand-built at Tamworth, but the upgraded SE5A (1972 to 1975) would be the best seller in a long line of Scimitars stretching ahead to 1995.

FIRST MANUFACTURED:
1968 (until 1972)
ENGINE:
2,553 cc Straight Six or 2,994 cc V6
PERFORMANCE:
With the V6 engine – top speed of 121 mph (195 km/h); 0-60 mph (97 km/h) in 8.9 secs
YOU SHOULD KNOW:
Many cars on both sides of the Atlantic were named after the sleek fighter aircraft of World War II, but it was surely a coincidence that the 1960s' Reliant Scimitar shared a designation with the SE5 – that fine British biplane that duelled with the Red Baron's Fokker Triplane in World War I.

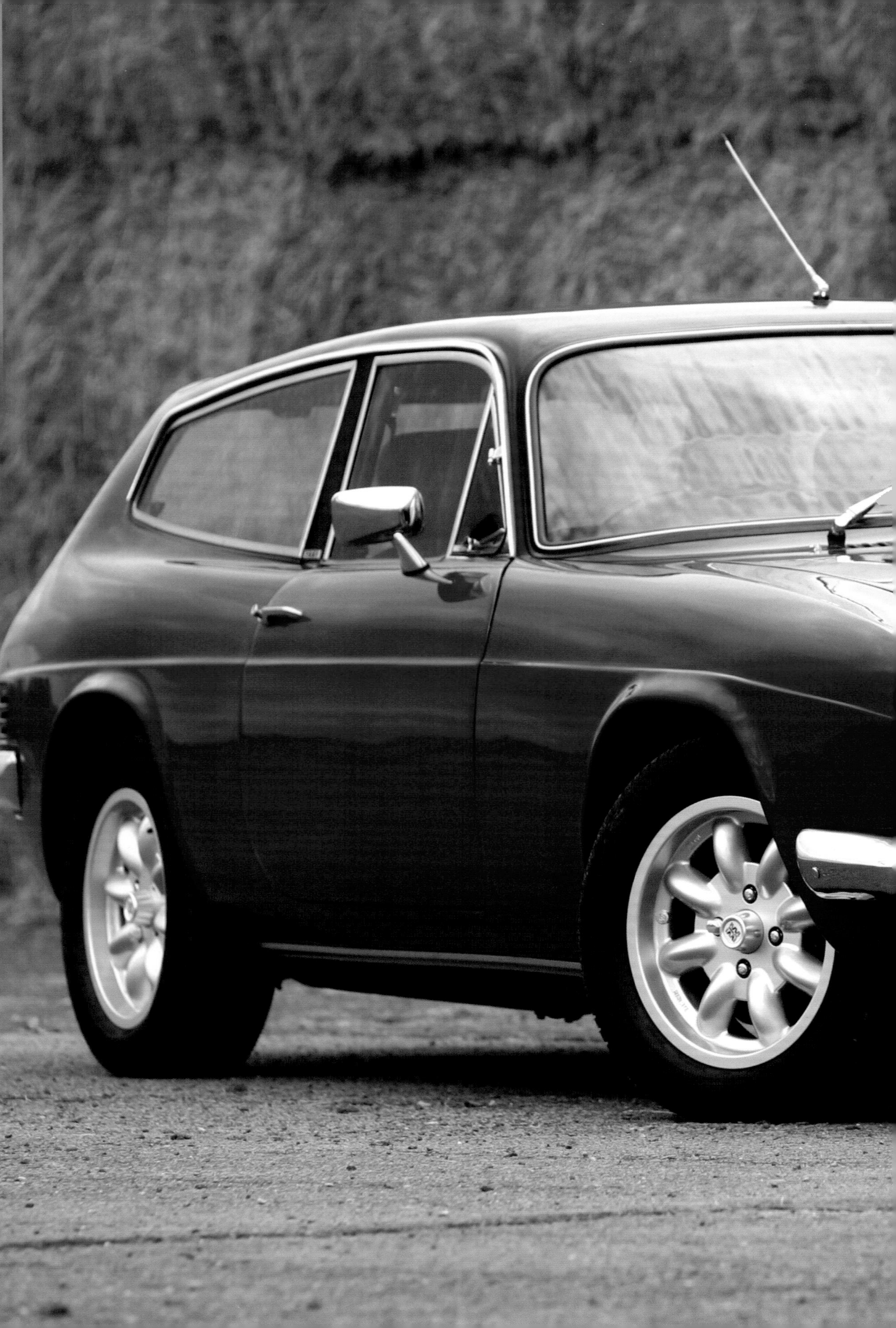

It is hard to believe that the Scimitar came from the same manufacturer that proposed the Reliant Robin economy cars.

The superb Silver Shadow proved to be the most successful Roller to date, doing extremely well commercially.

Rolls-Royce Silver Shadow

Neatly bisecting the 1960s, the Rolls-Royce Silver Shadow was introduced in October 1965 and would continue in production for more than a dozen years, becoming the most successful Roller ever made. The Silver Shadow had been in development for a considerable time and when this signature model appeared it incorporated many modern features that finally consigned some hitherto sacred Rolls-Royce design principles to history – along with the unwanted perception that Rolls-Royces were becoming rather old fashioned.

The new model no longer employed the traditional chassis beloved of custom coachbuilders, instead using monocoque construction. Suspension consisted of independent springing on all four wheels and four-wheel disc brakes to ensure smooth and effortless stopping power, even from the Silver Shadow's impressive top speed. This was achieved using the powerful 6.2 litre aluminium V8 carried forward from the Silver Cloud, coupled to an improved four-speed automatic gearbox, soon to be replaced with all-new three-speed torque transmission. There was an advanced hydraulic system (licensed from Citroen) that offered dual-circuit braking and self-levelling suspension, guaranteeing excellent ride quality. Naturally, the interior was discreetly palatial with the finest hide upholstery available in a choice of eight colours to tone with the 14 bodywork shades offered.

A long-wheelbase variant, sometimes with internal glass divider, was introduced in 1969. There was also a two-door fixed-head coupe model by Mulliner Park Ward or James Young, the latter much scarcer. A convertible followed in 1967 and this desirable model was given its own identity in 1971 as the Corniche. Much later, a Pininfarina coupe was built on the Shadow's platform and christened the Camargue, which was then the most expensive Roller of all, with a higher price than the Phantom VI limousine. Corniches and Camargues comfortably outlived their parent, with the last examples built in 1986.

FIRST MANUFACTURED:
1965 (until 1976)
ENGINE:
6,230 cc V8 (until 1970)
PERFORMANCE:
Top speed of 120 mph (193 mph);
0-60 mph (97 km/h) in 10.9 secs
YOU SHOULD KNOW:
Rolls-Royce produced a shared-platform Bentley T version that shadowed the Shadow all the way, also offering coupes and convertibles from Mulliner Park Ward and James Young – the only difference was the radiator grille, with the cheaper-to-make Bentley grille ensuring that the Silver Shadow was ever so slightly more expensive.

Rover P5B

The Rover P5 appeared in 1958, replacing the much-loved but elderly P4 (then a tired 25-year-old). The P5 was a larger car that took the Rover line up market, appealing as it did to successful businessmen and senior civil servants. It was also a very good car, soon becoming established as one of Britain's best-selling luxury motors of the 1960s.

The Mk I was powered by a 3 litre straight six. This solid four-door saloon had independent front suspension, whilst servo-assisted front discs soon became standard. Automatic transmission, overdrive on the manual box and power steering were options. A minor upgrade in 1961 saw front quarter lights introduced, but that was just a holding operation until the Mk II appeared in 1962. This featured better suspension and a tuned engine, also offering the choice of a coupe version with sporty lowered roofline. The Mk III of 1965 was little changed, though the styling was updated and the engine's power output further tweaked.

In 1967 the best P5 of all appeared – the P5B. The B stood for Buick, for Rover had taken the American company's unsuccessful lightweight aluminium V8 and improved it out of all recognition (indeed, evolutionary versions would remain around for decades). This engine gave the P5B lots more grunt, which was teamed with standard Borg-Warner automatic transmission and power steering. Not much changed externally, but a pair of fog lamps gave the front a magisterial four-light look and (lest anyone should doubt that this was the new model) chrome Rostyle wheels were complemented by prominent '3.5 Litre' badging.

The P5B has become a collectable modern classic, and still gives drivers a superior feeling as they glide effortlessly amongst lesser vehicles. The saloon was produced in the largest numbers, making the coupe rarer and therefore more desirable.

FIRST MANUFACTURED:
1967 (until 1973)
ENGINE:
3,528 cc V8
PERFORMANCE:
Coupe – top speed of 113 mph
(182 km/h)
YOU SHOULD KNOW:
The P5 may have remained as an aspirational purchase for the British middle classes, but was classy enough to be acceptable to Royalty and Prime Ministers – Queen Elizabeth II used one, as did PMs Harold Wilson, Edward Heath, James Callaghan and Margaret Thatcher.

The P5B seemed British through and through, but actually had a modified Buick V8 engine.

Rover 2000

FIRST MANUFACTURED:
1963 (until 1973)
ENGINE:
1,978 cc Straight Four
PERFORMANCE:
Rover 2000 TC – top speed of 112
mph (180 km/h); 0-60 mph (97 km/h)
in 9.9 secs
YOU SHOULD KNOW:
The rarest of P6s are the fewer than
200 that were converted to Estoura
estate cars with Rover's blessing, the
work being undertaken by H R Owen
and Crayford Engineering – though it is
thought that a minority of these were
actually based on Rover 2000s.

The P6 would be the last of Rover's P-classification model lines but – even after it was finally discontinued – not many people knew that, because the three P6 models were invariably known by their engine size – 2000, 2200 or 3500. The Rover 2000 replaced the P4 in 1963 and was an entirely new design. The somewhat angular shape was very different from its comfortably rounded predecessor but was very much in tune with the times, being voted European Car of the Year in 1964.

This was in part due to advanced features like an all-synchro gearbox, four-wheel disc brakes and de Dion tube rear suspension. The 2 litre overhead-cam engine had been specially designed for the P6 2000 with a flat Heron head that had combustion chambers let into the piston heads. This would be redesigned and fitted with twin SU carburettors for the 2000 TC, upping the power output by a quarter. This performance version had competed in rally competition and was primarily intended for export to America, though it was available on the home market from late '66.

The next evolution was the Rover 3500, which was launched in 1968 with the powerful aluminium V8 engine already used to good effect in the Rover P5. Both 2000 and 3500 were offered side by side, jointly seeing a major revision in 1970 with a Mk II version that delivered minor styling changes and an enhanced interior. The battery was moved to the boot, further encroaching on already limited luggage space.

The 2000 continued in production until the Rover 2200 appeared in 1973 with a bored-out version of the 2000 engine, allowing the 2000 to be honourably retired. Production of the entire P6 series finally came to an end in 1977 after a long and commercially successful run.

The Rover 2000 was a part of the last successful model line produced by a great British manufacturer that failed to move with the automotive times.

Sunbeam Tiger

The first car to bear the stand-alone Sunbeam name for more than 30 years was the old-fashioned Sunbeam Alpine roadster introduced by the Rootes Group in 1953 to cash in on the post-war British appetite for open-top motoring, but it didn't last long. The Alpine really came into its own after a complete revamp saw its launch as a new sports car in 1959. This had clean modern lines and would zip through the Swinging Sixties.

However, it was primarily intended for the important US export market, and a canny American sales executive suggested beefing up the basic 1.6 litre Series II Alpine to create something closer to high-powered muscle cars like the Shelby Cobra, then becoming popular in the States. This initiative saw Carroll Shelby himself create a prototype that contained the Cobra's 4.3 litre Ford Windsor V8 engine. A second example was created by Shelby associate Ken Miles and Rootes was persuaded that the idea could fly.

Further testing by Jensen Motors confirmed that the engineering sums added up, and the Sunbeam Tiger (built by Jensen at West Bromwich) made its growling appearance in 1964. It didn't look so very different from the gentler Alpine, but of course performance was in a different league.

Sadly, the Tiger adventure would not last long. Chrysler took over the Rootes Group in 1967, was not prepared to sell a car that had a Ford engine but couldn't provide a suitable Chrysler alternative. After just four years – and some 7,000 cars – production came to an end. Only some 500 of these were the second series Mk II cars with a larger engine, which are consequently the most desirable. But anyone lucky enough to catch any Tiger by the tail will appreciate how special this fast feline was.

It may have looked like any old Alpine, but as the name suggested this one really did have a tiger in its tank.

FIRST MANUFACTURED:
1964 (until 1967)
ENGINE:
4,261 cc or 5,306 cc V8
PERFORMANCE:
With 4.3 l engine – top speed
of 116 mph (187 km/h);
0-60 mph (97 km/h) in 9.5 secs
YOU SHOULD KNOW:
The name 'Tiger' was chosen for the beefed-up Alpine because it harked back to a great V12 Sunbeam racing car of the 1920s – driven by Sir Henry Seagrave, the Sunbeam Tiger was the first to exceed 150 mph (240 km/h), becoming a proud holder of the World Land Speed Record.

The Sunbeam Tiger made its growling appearance in 1964, but its adventure was short lived.

The Spitfire offered fun open-top motoring on a tight budget.

Triumph Spitfire Mk I

The Austin-Healey Sprite proved there was a market for small British sports cars and the bandwagon springs were soon creaking as first the MG Midget and then the Triumph Spitfire climbed aboard – both would outlast their inspiration, with the late-arriving Spitfire doing best with nearly 315,000 sold in 18 years. It evolved considerably during that run, but it all began with the Mk I (sometimes called the Spitfire 4) in 1962.

In fact, Standard-Triumph had been planning their baby sports car for some time, having commissioned a design in the late 1950s. It was based on the Triumph Herald saloon, which had a separate chassis that was easily modified to carry a sports body without the need for expensive retooling. Even so, the company couldn't afford to launch the Spitfire until Leyland took over.

The new owner discovered the traditionally styled prototype with its pleasing lines lurking in the Standard-Triumph factory and promptly sanctioned production. This basic sports car had advantages – like a tilt-forward front end that offered excellent access to the 1.1 litre engine – and disadvantages like swing-axle rear suspension that was liable to cause violent oversteer. Trim was basic, though the Spitfire had wind-up windows (unlike contemporary Sprites and Midgets) whilst wire wheels and a hard top were options.

The Triumph Spitfire went through several evolutions. There was a GT6 coupe from 1966 to 1973. The Spitfire Mk II (1965–1967) saw a relatively minor interim upgrade. The Mk III (1967–1970) had a serious facelift with a bigger engine. The Mk IV (1970–1974) saw a major upgrade with significant style changes. The last version was the Spitfire 1500, with the largest engine of all, which ran from 1974 to 1980, though not without problems – completing a series that offered fun-packed, affordable open-top motoring.

FIRST MANUFACTURED:
1962 (until 1980)
ENGINE:
1,147 cc Straight Four
PERFORMANCE:
Top speed of 92 mph (148 km/h);
0-60 mph (97 km/h) in 17.3 secs
YOU SHOULD KNOW:
The final demise of the Triumph Spitfire in 1980 ended an era, as Standard-Triumph's historic works at Canley, Coventry, was closed shortly afterwards – and after passing through various hands the Triumph name finished up being owned by BMW, which kept the name after selling on the Rover Group.

Triumph Vitesse Mk II

By the late 1950s Standard-Triumph was experiencing financial difficulty, though TR sports cars were thriving, as the company's small Standard saloons had never sold well. So the Triumph Herald was introduced to replace those ageing Standards. Italian Giovanni Michelotti designed the pretty little two-door saloon with lots of glass, which had an old-fashioned rolling chassis to which the body was bolted. This had the advantage of allowing different body styles to be used without much difficulty and a coupe, convertible, estate car and van soon appeared.

If there was one problem it was that the Herald – with its small engine – was not the zippiest of performers. Standard-Triumph's answer was to create the Vitesse 6. Also by Michelotti, it mostly used Herald body panels and had a distinctive front with two pairs of slanting headlights. Power was supplied by a 1.5 litre straight six, modified from the Standard Vanguard Six engine. Saloons and convertibles were offered and the level of interior trim was high. The compact Vitesse 6 appeared in 1962 and was soon being uprated. The first big evolution was the Vitesse 2 Litre of 1966, but the more powerful car highlighted a generic weakness in Triumph's performance models – rear suspension that caused serious oversteer under hard driving.

Triumph finally solved this problem – and created an excellent car – with the Vitesse Mk II, launched in 1968. The new suspension system guaranteed leech-like roadholding and the tweaked engine delivered performance that could put the enhanced handling to a proper test. Again, there were both saloon and convertible versions, and it was the latter that represented terrific value for the sporting motorist who liked the thrill of open-top driving. It was a handsome four-seater that could easily outperform contemporary sports cars like the MGB, and remains extremely collectable to this day.

FIRST MANUFACTURED:
1968 (until 1971)
ENGINE:
1,998 cc Straight Six
PERFORMANCE:
Top speed of 100 mph (140 km/h);
0-60 mph (97 km/h) in 11.2 secs
YOU SHOULD KNOW:
Just over 9,000 Vitesse Mk IIs were produced in four years, with the saloon selling around 5,600 and convertible some 3,500 – and there is a definite scarcity of earlier Vitesse cars as many have been cannibalized for spares to keep the ultra-desirable Mk II compact sports models going.

The Vitesse represented terrific value for the sporting motorist, combining style with power and great roadholding.

Triumph TR6

FIRST MANUFACTURED:
1969 (until 1976)
ENGINE:
2.498 cc Straight Six
PERFORMANCE:
Top speed of 118mph (191 km/h);
0-60 mph (97 km/h) in around
9.5 secs
YOU SHOULD KNOW:
The TR6's fuel-injected engine failed US
emissions requirements so models for
export to America were
a somewhat strangulated
twin-carburetted version.

'Rattly, draughty, unpredictable in the wet, prone to disintegration . . .' That's how celebrity car buff, James May described the TR6. And coming from him, the words were glowing praise; for it is the sheer, unadulterated blokishness of the TR6 that was the secret of its success – a hunky machine, modelled along the lines of a classic British roadster but with the promise of high-performance tearaway thrills. When it came onto the market it immediately hit the spot, and by the time production ended in 1976 the TR6 was Triumph's best seller – more than 94,500 had been built.

The TR6 was the consummation of a series that had evolved steadily through each model. Mechanically more or less identical to the TR5 (which itself was simply a TR4 with a pushrod six-cylinder engine) the TR6 had a classy new body, styled by Karmann. Its flowing lines gave it a beautiful old-fashioned shape and the interior had touches of opulence: pile carpet, wooden dashboard and

comfortable bucket seats with plenty of leg room. A steel hardtop
was included as an optional extra for instant conversion to a sports
coupe. Built in Triumph's Coventry factory using the traditional
body-on-frame construction method rather than the mass-production
unibody technology that by then had become the norm, the TR6
had four-speed manual transmission with optional overdrive, rack-
and-pinion steering and a fuel-injected engine – which gave so much
power that Triumph had to detune it from 150 bhp to 125 bhp to
make it more manageable.

The TR6 is a brilliant hobbyist's car for weekend tinkering.
Spare parts are readily available and inexpensive, the electrics are
straightforward and there is enough room around the engine to wield
a spanner with ease. And on the road, it fulfils every criterion of
those boy racer dreams – a superb heritage toy.

*The distinctive TR6 remains
an enduring favourite with the
classic sports car fraternity.*

Vanden Plas Princess 4 Litre

Vanden Plas was a coachbuilding company that originated in Belgium and was licensed in the United Kingdom from 1910. After various ups and downs the British company built Bentley bodies in the 1920s, then worked for various makers including Alvis, Daimler and Rolls-Royce in the 1930s. After World War II Vanden Plas was acquired by Austin, which gave Vanden Plas the job of fitting bodies to the upmarket A135 Princess. From 1960 Austin successor BMC decided that Vanden Plas should be a stand-alone marque, so the Austin Princess turned into the stately Vanden Plas Princess 4 Litre.

This hand-built luxury limousine went through two generations before the Vanden Plas marque was abolished, with the name subsequently being used for top-of-the-range models by various companies within the merged British Leyland Motor Corporation from 1968, including Jaguar. The Princess 4 Litre had a relatively short life and was eventually replaced by the Daimler DS420, Leyland's sole limousine offering.

The Princess was beautifully made, gave a super-comfortable ride and came with the added bonus of a Rolls-Royce engine.

The first Vanden Plas Princess 4 Litre was the former Austin Princess IV, which had been restyled in 1956 to eliminate the car's dated look though mechanicals were not much changed. These ceremonial limos were never big sellers (just 200 in nine years), but the Vanden Plas Princess 4 Litre R was a different story, with nearly 7,000 made between its launch in 1964 and the demise of Vanden Plas as independent marque.

This was an interesting vehicle as the Princess 4 Litre R had a Rolls-Royce straight six under the bonnet (signified by the 'R'). It possessed more rounded styling than its predecessor and lost the tail fins. It had the distinction of being the only mass-produced passenger car ever to have a Rolls-Royce engine and was something of a favourite with politicians, senior government officials and up-and-coming businessmen.

FIRST MANUFACTURED:
1960 (until 1968)
ENGINE:
3,995 cc or 3,909 cc Straight Six
PERFORMANCE:
Princess 4 Litre R – top speed of
106 mph (171 km/h)
YOU SHOULD KNOW:
The only other model Vanden Plas built
in its own name was the Pininfarina-
designed car simply known as the
Vanden Plas Princess
– it was a luxury four-door saloon built
from 1960 to 1964 that had a 2.9 litre
engine and was based on the Austin
A99 Westminster.

1970s

AC 3000ME

Go looking for a crock of gold at the end of the nearest rainbow and you'll probably find it just before you manage to locate an AC 3000ME – just one hundred of these low-slung cars were built and they tended to rust. It all came about because AC boss Derek Hurlock was looking for a small custom-built luxury car with which to tackle the fuel-starved 1970s, and found the one-off Diablo prototype built by racing privateers Robin Stables and Peter Bohanna around an Austin Maxi engine. AC bought the rights and started developing it as the 3000ME.

After somewhat prematurely showing an 3000ME mid-engined concept car containing the Ford Essex V6 engine at the 1973 Earls Court Motor Show in London, AC hit trouble when new regulations called for a crash test – which the 3000ME failed in 1976 at the very point when it was ready for sale. A major reworking of the chassis secured an A+ in the crash test, but AC's limited resources meant

Technical difficulties and new regulations delayed the arrival of the 3000ME for years.

that the uprated and improved car did not manage to go to market until 1979. When it did, the wait must have seemed worthwhile for those lucky enough to secure one.

With its thrusting wedge-shaped front end, distinctive air intakes and advanced features, this was a handsome high-performance coupe with exceptional roadholding in best AC traditions. It had pop-up headlamps, five-speed gearbox, independent suspension and disc brakes all round. AC also included goodies like adjustable steering column, electric windows, sunshine roof, sun-dym laminated windscreen and windows, through-flow ventilation, electric aerial, alloy wheels and stainless steel exhaust. This was a terrific little car, but production delays meant the 3000ME arrived too late – the problem of competing with the formidable Lotus Esprit was insurmountable and production ceased at the Thames Ditton facility in 1984.

FIRST MANUFACTURED:
1979 (until 1984)
ENGINE:
2,994 cc OHV V6
PERFORMANCE:
Top speed of 120 mph (193 km/h);
0-60 mph (97 km/h) in 8.5 secs
YOU SHOULD KNOW:
The last AC 3000MEs were built north of the border after the AC name and car were licensed to the AC (Scotland) company formed for the purpose – but only 30 more cars were built at the factory in Hillington, Glasgow, before the new enterprise failed in 1985.

The Vantage V8 looked the part and delivered on its promises.

Aston Martin Vantage V8

It was quite a responsibility to be named 'Britain's First Supercar', but the 1977 Vantage V8 was up for it with the ability to beat a Ferrari Daytona to 60 mph (97 km/h) from a standing start and with a stratospheric top speed. Aston Martin had used the Vantage name before, usually to indicate a high-performance version of an existing model, and the Vantage V8 was a souped-up version of the regular Aston Martin V8 – itself effectively the DBS V8 relaunched in 1972.

However, this time the Vantage was classified as a model in its own right. Tadek Marek's excellent V8 engine was tuned to deliver 438 bhp with increased compression, large inlet valves, special camshafts, new manifolds and enlarged carburettors – a set-up that would remain until an engine upgrade in 1986.

The Vantage was distinguishable from the standard V8 by its rear spoiler, blanked-out radiator grille and closed-off bonnet without an air scoop. The Vantage also had flared wheel arches and side skirts (though Prince Charles ordered one without the latter embellishments, setting a minor fashion). There were various small styling and wheel changes throughout the Vantage V8's long life. Two versions were offered – the saloon (313 produced) and the fabulous Volante convertible (115 built), the Volante not being introduced until 1987.

And yes, James Bond did indeed drive an imaginary Aston Martin Vantage V8 in *The Living Daylights*. It was actually three cars meant to be one – a V8 Vantage Volante convertible and two non-Vantage V8 saloons – with bulletproof windows, fireproof bodywork, retractable outriggers, wheel lasers, heat-seeking missiles, an afterburner, tyre spikes and a self-destruct system. All that said, most people would love to slip behind the wheel of any old Aston Martin Vantage V8 and have a licence to be thrilled.

FIRST MANUFACTURED:
1986 (until 1988)
ENGINE:
5,341 cc V8
PERFORMANCE:
Top speed of 186 mph (300 km/h);
0-60 mph (97 km/h) in 4.8 secs
YOU SHOULD KNOW:
The years 1985–1990 saw the peak of 'silly money' supercars. Most of the 50 Aston Martin V8 Zagatos produced were bought by investors who merely stored them in the expectation of huge profits (prices reached £500,000). Consequently, the car is a very rare sight indeed. Those buyers missed the point completely – the V8 Zagato is enormous fun, a true driving machine.

Ford Escort Mexico

One of the clever evolutions of the Ford Escort Mk 1 was the Mexico road car. The works team's Ford Escort RS1600s won the Daily Mirror World Cup Rally in 1970 and also finished third, fifth and sixth. The winning car was driven by Hannu Mikkola and Gunnar Palm who conquered a gruelling 16,000 mile (25,750 km) course through Europe and South America, starting at London's Wembley Stadium in mid-April and finishing in Mexico City during late May.

This extraordinary event attracted massive public interest, and Ford was a past master at turning motor-racing victories into hard cash by selling road cars that exploited the cachet of competition success. It was therefore no surprise to anyone when the distinctive Escort Mexico started appearing in showrooms up and down Britain. In fact, this custom version wasn't really so very different from any old Escort Mk 1, but that didn't stop it becoming a popular buy with dedicated motorsports enthusiasts.

The Escort Mexico did have the robust Ford Kent OHV engine, and shared the competition RS1600's strengthened two-door body shell, plus Rallye Sport suspension and brakes. Buyers obviously wanted to trumpet the fact that they had a special car, so the Mexico sported bucket seats and wide body stripes that contrasted with the rest of the paintwork. Extras like alloy wheels and four rather ostentatiously covered rally-style spotlamps on the front usually completed the impressive picture.

Escort Mexicos have become very desirable amongst those who like to own, maintain and drive collectable British cars from the 1970s. They are affordable, robust, easy to work on and still drive well. And with fewer than 10,000 produced during the four-year production run, the Mexico stands out from the large crowd of Escort Mk 1s that have dodged the scrapyard.

FIRST MANUFACTURED:
1970 (until 1974)
ENGINE:
1,599 cc OHV Straight Four
PERFORMANCE:
Top speed of 100 mph (161 km/h);
0-50 mph (80 km/h) in 7.9 secs
YOU SHOULD KNOW:
The Mk 2 Escort Mexico was produced between 1975 and 1978 and is much rarer than its predecessor, having to compete with the Escort 1600 Sport and the pokey Escort RS2000 – just 2,500 examples were built at Saarlouis in West Germany.

Ford won the gruelling World Cup Rally in 1970 and soon cashed in with a successful road car that ticked all the right commercial boxes.

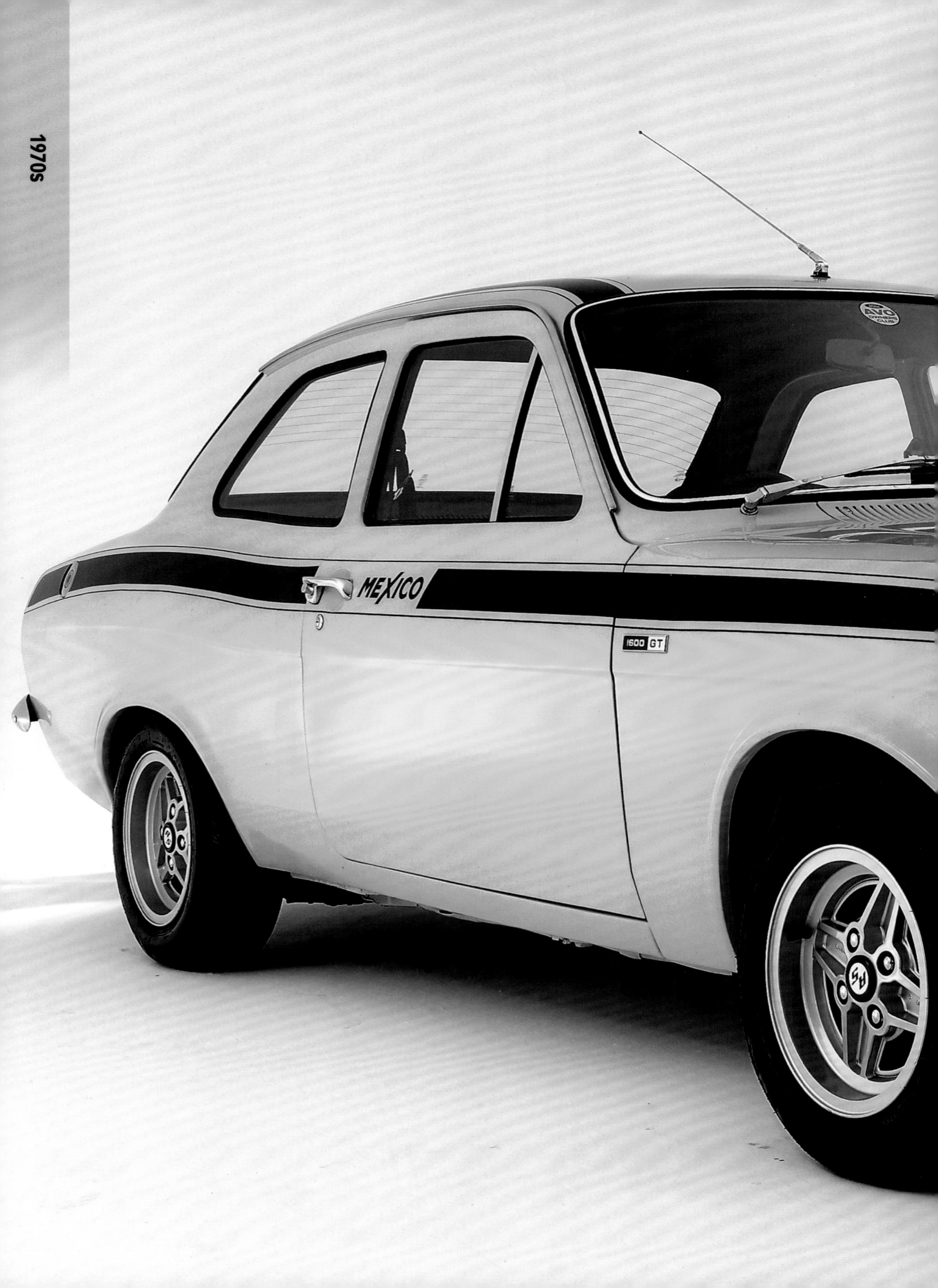
MEXICO
1600 GT

Affordable, robust and easy to work on, the Ford Mexico is a very desirable car for all 1970s' enthusiasts.

Ford Escort RS1600

Technically this may be a variation of the Escort Mk I, but the Ford Escort RS1600 is a distinctive predator that would feel insulted to be lumped together with its decent but undoubtedly tamer siblings. For this was the fearsome competition car that battered the opposition into almost total submission from the early 1970s.

It was fairly obvious that the RS1600 was not designed for gently commuting to the station.

And it was the first car to wear Ford's RS (for Rallye Sport) badge of honour, which would frequently speed to race wins in the decades ahead. Some 20 wildly different cars have been RS-badged since the Escort RS1600 appeared in 1970 – but the accolade is not awarded lightly, strictly reserved for competition-hardened thoroughbreds. Ford tries to ensure that road-going RS cars offer advanced technology, great performance, terrific roadholding and value for money.

This winning formula was pioneered by the Escort RS1600, the first Ford to use a 16-valve twin overhead-camshaft engine. It was also first to be assembled at the company's new AVO (Advanced Vehicle Operation) factory at Aveley. The impressive hat trick was the RS1600's status as the first car to be sold through a specialist network of Rallye Sport dealerships.

The RS1600 was developed from the Escort Mk 1 twin-cam and was fitted with a 1.6 litre BDA 16-valve engine. Stiffened body shells, sports suspension and front disc brakes helped cope with the rigorous demands of long-distance rallies. In fact, for the longest events 1860 pushrod X-flow engines replaced the BDAs, as the robust replacement never suffered mechanical failure. Road versions were detuned compared to works racers, but still offered (and still do offer) high speed coupled with punchy acceleration to thrill sporting drivers.

With the advent of the Escort Mk 2 in 1976, the RS1600 morphed into the RS1800 – an even more potent machine that would consolidate Ford's hard-earned racing reputation.

FIRST MANUFACTURED:
1970 (until 1975)
ENGINE:
1,599 cc DOHC Straight Four
PERFORMANCE:
Road version – top speed of 113 mph (182 km/h); 0-50 mph (80 km/h) in 6.4 secs
YOU SHOULD KNOW:
Impressive competition scalps lifted by the awesome RS1600 included the East African Safari Rally of 1972, three RAC Rallies and the European Touring Car Championship of 1974.

Jaguar XJ-S Mk I

Replacing a 20th-century icon when the E-Type was finally discontinued was always going to be a thankless task – and so it proved. Jaguar's replacement for its phenomenal sports car was a very different animal – the XJ-S Mk I. This 2+2 coupe was based on the XJ Saloon and was more of a luxurious grand tourer than out-and-out sports car, though a fuel-injected 5.3 litre V12 engine inherited from the E-Type ensured that the XJ-S had supercar performance.

Even so, it never captured the public's affection as its predecessor had, perhaps because the styling was not to everyone's taste. Although it was a big car, the XJ-S was loosely designed along American ponycar lines – low and wide, with a long bonnet and short rear deck, divided by a fastback cabin. At first the XJ-S Mk I came with a manual gearbox option but that sporty choice was soon discontinued, leaving three-speed automatic transmission as standard.

The XJ-S may have been different from the E-Type, but it certainly delivered within its own terms of reference. Many now consider it to be the best GT of its generation, with superb ride quality and impeccable handling. The combination of strong performance and effortless refinement was seductive, and the XJ-S sold well.

Around 14,800 XJ-S Mk Is were built before the Mk II arrived in 1981, with its improved high-efficiency V12 and 3.6 litre straight six variant. The early cars went through hard times as they worked their way down the used-car pyramid from luxury grand tourer to expensive-to-run rust bucket. But the passage of time has been kind to perception of those that remain. Although still not as popular as the Mk II cars with their targa and convertible variations, early Mk Is are starting to be collected and restored as future classics.

FIRST MANUFACTURED:
1975 (until 1980)
ENGINE:
5,344 cc V12
PERFORMANCE:
Top speed of 150 mph (240 km/h);
0-60 mph (97 km/h) in 6.9 secs
YOU SHOULD KNOW:
Responding to criticism that the XJ-S was a somewhat dull successor to the slender E-Type visually, Jaguar commissioned Pininfarina to design the Jaguar XJ Spider concept car, but never put this flamboyant machine into production.

The E-Type replacement had an impossible act to follow but has gradually acquired a good reputation as a minor GT classic.

Jensen-Healey

When the Austin-Healey 3000 was discontinued, Kjell Qvale was disappointed. The entrepreneurial Californian had built up a massive business importing and selling British and European performance cars in the USA. As such he was an influential player, managing to persuade Donald Healey and Jensen Motors to design and build a sports car to fill the hole left by the late, lamented 3000.

The project was actioned and the result appeared in 1972. The Jensen-Healey was a traditional roadster, created with sourced components like running gear from the Vauxhall Firenza, Sunbeam Rapier transmission and front brakes that originated from the truly awful Morris Marina. The suspension was simple but effective – live rear axle with coils and trailing arms coupled with double wishbone and coil springs at the front. The car had drum brakes at the rear and discs up front. Interiors were functional.

Poor build quality severely compromised Jensen-Healey's commercial prospects.

After experimenting with various different engines, it was decided that the Jensen-Healey should use the brand-new Lotus 907, a DOHC 16-valve all-alloy motor. This was teamed with a four- or five-speed manual gearbox to deliver impressive performance – though as always the package had to be detuned to meet US emission control regulations. It was also an American requirement that unattractive rubber bumpers should be fitted (from 1974).

Kjell Qvale did his part, ensuring that the sporty Jensen-Healey sold well in the States. But all was not well on the home front. The 1973 oil crisis had virtually killed off the thirsty Jensen Interceptor, and the company scrambled to fill the void by developing the Jensen GT, a sporting estate-car version of the roadster. This was a terrific little speedster, but only a few hundred were made before Jensen folded in 1976, leaving behind a legacy of around 10,000 Jensen-Healey models to tempt future sports car collectors.

FIRST MANUFACTURED:
1972 (until 1976)
ENGINE:
1,973 cc DOHC Straight Four
PERFORMANCE:
Top speed of 119 mph (192 km/h);
0-60 mph (97 km/h) in 7.8 secs
YOU SHOULD KNOW:
A factory-sponsored Jensen-Healey team went sports car racing in America during 1973 and 1974, winning the SCCA (Sports Car Club of America) D Production Championship in both years. But this commendable effort ended in 1975 ahead of Jensen Motors' collapse.

Lotus Esprit

The long-running success story that was the Esprit started as a production spin-off from a concept car designed by Giorgetto Giugiaro. It was among the first of his renowned 'folded paper' cars, a clean-lined, sharp-angled wedge in the forefront of fashion. Colin Chapman, with the luxury supercar market in mind, immediately snapped up the design for Lotus. When the Esprit first appeared in 1976 it was somewhat disparagingly labelled a 'poor man's Ferrari' but it soon acquired snob appeal by appearing as James Bond's vehicle in *The Spy Who Loved Me* (1977) epitomizing British 1970s' glamour – powerful, exclusive, stylish, and (not least) a lot more reliable than a Ferrari.

The Esprit S1 was a mid-engine, high-performance two-door coupe with a GRP (glass-reinforced plastic) body built on a steel backbone chassis, weighing in at less than 1000 kg (2200 lbs).

It's true, it's true – the great British Esprit proved that Italy didn't have a supercar monopoly.

Lotus used pre-existing parts to keep costs down and fitted a Lotus 907 lightweight alloy 2 litre engine with twin cams and 16 valves. From the start the car was praised for its superb handling, though there was the occasional gripe about insufficient power, especially in the USA where the engine was downrated to comply with emissions regulations.

Over the years, the Lotus Esprit went through several incarnations with a couple of major revamps. The body was restyled with rounder features in 1987 and was remodelled again in 1993, and throughout the 28 years of its production, continual mechanical improvements were made to enhance performance. All these tweakings have added to the original Giugiaro model's legendary status. The very last model was the 1999 Sport 350, which could do 0-60 mph (97 km/h) in less than 5 secs, but it is the 1976 Giugiaro S1 design that will be remembered as the iconic supercar of its era.

FIRST MANUFACTURED:
1976 (until 2004)
ENGINE:
1,973 cc, 2,174 cc Slant Four
(1976–1996)
PERFORMANCE:
Top speed around 130 mph
(209 km/h); 0-60 mph (97km/h)
in 8 secs
YOU SHOULD KNOW:
Altogether 10,675 Esprits were produced over the course of its 28-year run. Some models are extremely rare. To celebrate Lotus's success on the racetrack, an exclusive gold and black JPS (John Player Special) model was produced in a run of less than 150, and a mere 45 special red, blue and chrome 'Essex' versions of the 1980 turbocharged Esprit were made.

The Mantis M70 was a bizarre entry in the supercar lexicon – and an exceedingly rare animal.

Marcos Mantis M70

From its inception in 1959, Marcos had been associated with the race track rather than the road. The company's founders, engineers Jem Marsh and Frank Costin made a name for themselves among the racing fraternity by building cars that, although not always beautiful, performed outstandingly well. Costin's experience in the aero industry gave the company an edge in pioneering wooden-chassised unibody technology to produce remarkably powerful lightweight cars.

The first Mantis was built in 1968: a mid-engine racer that was a one-off. It was an apt name – the futuristic design was reminiscent of nothing so much as a giant predatory insect. After racing it only once, Jem Marsh fitted it with a new engine suitable for road use before selling it in the USA. But the name was too good to waste on a single car that had disappeared to the other side of the Atlantic so when Marcos decided to branch out into mainstream car manufacture with its 2+2 road tourer, the 'Mantis' label was recycled. The Mantis M70 was unveiled at the 1970 Earl's Court Motor Show to be met with gaping stares. Nobody knew quite what to make of its startlingly brazen design – a fantastical long-nosed monster built in GRP and fitted with a Triumph TR6 fuel-injected engine.

Who knows whether the Mantis would have been a triumphant success under different circumstances but Marcos was plagued by production problems and financial difficulties which led to the company's collapse after only 32 of these amazing sports coupes had been built. The Mantis M70 was the only four-seater car that Marcos produced. If you even glimpse one you're lucky, and if by some amazing good fortune you get a chance to have a go in it, grab the opportunity for the rarity value alone.

FIRST MANUFACTURED:
1970 (until 1971)
ENGINE:
2,498 cc Straight Six
PERFORMANCE:
Top speed of 120 mph (193 km/h);
0-60 mph (97 km/h) in 8 secs
YOU SHOULD KNOW:
Over the years the Marcos company was beset by financial difficulties and after two relaunches it finally folded for good in 2007.

Panther de Ville

The growing 1970s' appetite for replicas was largely confined to smaller kit or factory-built sports cars, until the English manufacturer Panther Westwinds set a new trend for powerful, luxury automobiles styled on the panache of the 'Golden Age' of the 1930s. Panther's first car was the J72, a replica of Jaguar's SS100. Its phenomenal success persuaded Panther to attempt something even more spectacular. The Panther de Ville four-door saloon of 1974 was a glorious whiff of a 1930 Bugatti Royale. It was no imitation – but the de Ville gave a brilliant impression of a Bugatti, with the long sweep of its wings and running boards culminating in an imposing arch of a front grille, enormous headlights, and a sporty tilt to the windscreen. Only the design of its two-tone paintwork was actually copied from Bugatti. What you can't see immediately is the Jaguar underneath that made the Panther de Ville so easy to drive, so quick, and such fun. The giant wheelbase carried Jaguar suspension, power steering and automatic transmission, and a choice of either 4.2 litre or 5.3 litre engine. Hawk-eyed car buffs will also notice that the doors come from an Austin Maxi (BMC 1800).

If it was cobbled together, the Panther de Ville was meticulously hand-crafted to the highest standard. The interiors went beyond lavish to theatrical, with walnut and silver-appointed bars (including ice-maker) and TV, and a catalogue of refinements that encapsulated the ostentation of the era. Its opulence was worthy of an emperor (it was bought by Sir Elton John among others); yet it had a rakish, dangerous splendour like its Bugatti inspiration. Only 60 were made, including seven two-seat convertibles – and just one, six-door, turbo-charged, pink and gold limousine, festooned with headlights. Nicknamed 'The Golden Eagle', it was made for a Malaysian prince.

FIRST MANUFACTURED:
1974 (until 1984)
ENGINE:
4,235 cc Straight Six or 5,343 cc V12
PERFORMANCE:
Top speed of 150 mph (241 km/h);
0-60 mph (97 km/h) in 6.5 secs
YOU SHOULD KNOW:
The Panther de Ville was – naturally – the transport of choice of Cruella de Vil (played by Glenn Close) in Disney's films *101 Dalmatians* and *102 Dalmatians*.

Panther hoped to create a niche market for the de Ville but only 60 were ever made.

Range Rover Classic

If ever there was an accidental success story it's that of the Range Rover Classic. It was introduced in 1970 for the English county set, in the belief that a robust four-wheel drive vehicle that was more comfortable than the utilitarian Land Rover would go down well with those who rode horses, shot birds, hunted, attended agricultural shows and were always surrounded by wet dogs. As such, the first Range Rovers had vinyl seats and plastic dashboards that could be hosed down after green wellies tramped mud into the car.

Early two-door Range Rovers were built to deliver real cross-country ability. They had permanent four-wheel drive with low range for off-road work. Rover's V8 petrol engine was teamed with a four-speed manual gearbox. Advanced independent suspension offered coil springs all round with disc brakes front and back. To British Leyland's credit, they soon realized their new rural transport was appealing to a wider market, meeting the dual requirement of looking good and operating well both on and off the road.

This marked the start of enhancement and uprating that would last for decades, resulting in the creation of the ultimate luxury SUV that European manufacturers like BMW, Volkswagen and Porsche

FIRST MANUFACTURED:
1970 (until 1996) (first generation)
ENGINE:
3,532 cc, 3,947 cc or 4,197 cc V8; 2,393 cc or 2,499 cc Straight Four Diesel; 2,495 cc Straight Four Turbo-Diesel
PERFORMANCE:
With 3.5 l engine – top speed of 96 mph (154 km/h); 0-50 mph (80 km/h) in 11.1 secs
YOU SHOULD KNOW:
The series name was devised with the benefit of hindsight – Range Rover Classic was the tag used for first generation cars that briefly continued to be built alongside second generation cars in the 1990s, and Rover liked the name so much it retro-fitted the 'Classic' designation to all first generation Range Rovers.

eventually felt they had to challenge with their own awesome off-roaders primarily intended for imposing road use by wealthy drivers.

During the 1970s the Range Rover saw refinements like power steering introduced, but it was not until the early 1980s that significant change happened – including a four-door body and automatic transmission option. There were further style tweaks in the 1980s, plus innovations like the availability of diesel engines. A luxurious Vogue special edition was offered from 1983, and a stretched LSE model appeared in 1992. After 25 great years, second generation cars finally superseded the Range Rover Classic in 1996.

The Range Rover soon moved from the county set's favourite mode of transport to a more cosmopolitan appeal.

Reliant Bond Bug

FIRST MANUFACTURED:
1970 (until 1974)
ENGINE:
701 cc OHV Straight Four
PERFORMANCE:
Top speed of 75 mph (121 km/h)
YOU SHOULD KNOW:
When a new 750 cc Reliant Robin was launched in 1973, the Bond Bug 700s were dropped in favour of 750 E and ES versions. Apart from the larger engine, these were more or less identical to the earlier models. It is estimated that there are fewer than 900 Bond Bugs of any sort still in existence.

The Reliant Robin, Regal and Rialto three-wheeler cars have a certain air of eccentricity, a peculiarly British charm that is inextricably linked to 'characters' like Mr Bean, or Del Boy in the TV series *Only Fools and Horses*. Reliant was keen to dissociate three-wheelers from this rather whimsical image and wanted to promote them instead as sporty, fun cars for the young. With this in mind, the company commissioned Tom Karen of Ogle Design to work on a prototype. When, in 1969, Reliant took over its rival, the Bond Motor Co, it immediately stopped production of Bond cars and used the Bond factory solely to manufacture its own Ogle car. Although the Ogle was soon moved to Reliant's own workshops, the company marketed its new model under the Bond name.

The Bond Bug was a triangular fibreglass wedge built on a modified Reliant Regal chassis with the same mechanics and 0.7 litre part alloy engine. Instead of doors, the top of the car (including the side frames) was a hinged overhead canopy for people to climb in and out like pilots. The Bug came in three versions: the 700 – a very basic model without sidescreens; the 700E, which made slightly more concessions to comfort; and the 700 ES, a de luxe version with a higher compression engine, racing steering wheel, mud flaps and wing mirrors, and the generous inclusion of a spare wheel. In terms of power, the Bug matched a small four-wheeler but it was pricier than the Mini, which meant it was bound to fail. Only 2,268 Bugs were built (all painted a virulent shade of orange except for the six white versions that were made as a special promotion for Rothman's cigarettes). Unsurprisingly, this quirky little car now has a fanatical following and is much sought after.

Plastic, orange and short of a wheel – but at least drivers didn't need a full car licence.

Rolls-Royce Corniche

The Corniche had a late baptism in 1971. The monocoque construction of the 1965 Silver Shadow range made it virtually impossible for traditional coachbuilders to practise their calling: there was no separate chassis on which to fit panel work. Rolls-Royce faced the problem by increasing their stake in Mulliner Park Ward (MPW), already their in-house specialist partner, in order to develop a two-door coupe (1966) and two-door convertible (1967) based on the Silver Shadow. By 1971, with Rolls-Royce in the throes of splitting the company into separate divisions to solve a financial crisis, the time was ripe for the publicity splash of a new model. Both coupe and convertible were revamped and powered up, and launched as the Rolls-Royce (and, of course, Bentley) Corniche.

MPW learned how to press panels and weld them to the Silver Shadow floorpan. After technical assembly by Rolls-Royce in Crewe, which included the major modifications that justified the Corniche as an independent series, MPW completed the cars back in London. The hand-built quality showed, even if the 1971 'production' car didn't look very different. The sumptuous luxury extended to the finest detail, like the power-operated soft top which, alone, took as long as two weeks to make, fit and adjust. The bodyline still had the dip over the rear wheel arch that suggested the sporty monster sitting, poised on its athletic haunches.

You couldn't see many internal changes, but you could drive them. The Corniche wasn't about top speed, but about shifting its magnificent bulk with incomparably smooth ease, no matter what kind of road, throughout the low, mid and upper-mid ranges. Its stylish, measured glide became the benchmark of comfortable cruising. It was, literally as well as figuratively, designed for the Corniche. Monte Carlo and California absolutely adored it.

FIRST MANUFACTURED:
1971 (until 1982 Coupe);
(until 1987 Convertible)
ENGINE:
6,750 cc V8
PERFORMANCE:
Top speed of 125 mph (201 km/h);
0-60 mph (97 km/h) in 10.2 secs
YOU SHOULD KNOW:
When Rolls-Royce first experimented with what would become the Corniche, the celebrated coachbuilder James Young designed his own version alongside that of MPW. It never went into production, and the few Rollers made to Young's imaginative genius are among the rarest of the rare.

It was true what they said – if you had to ask the price of a Corniche you probably couldn't afford to buy one.

*The magnificently luxurious
Camargue was the ultimate
Roller.*

Rolls-Royce Camargue

The Camargue stands slightly apart, and indeed aloof, from other Rolls Royce series and models. The company had been inspired by a 1968 Bentley T unmistakably designed by that genius of Italian sports car styling, Pininfarina. Submerged in financial crisis during the early 1970s, Rolls-Royce needed a dramatic statement car. For the first time since World War II, a production model was not to be designed in-house. The new, top-of-the-range Rolls-Royce flagship was to be a really exclusive, two-door saloon styled with Pininfarina's impeccable elegance and sporty Italian panache. Longer and wider than the Corniche (long since available), the Camargue was nevertheless beautifully proportioned. The front grille was especially broad, and for the first time it was set at an oblique angle (7 degrees) to match the snappier inclines of the front and rear screens. The window glass itself was curved – another first for Rolls-Royce, along with the revolutionary automatic split-level air-conditioning (which cost as much as a Mini, took 8 years to develop, and had the cooling capacity of 30 refrigerators) envied throughout the automotive world.

Mechanically, the Camargue was much the same as the Corniche and Silver Shadow. It was a little more powerful – but it was still a coupe, albeit the largest and most luxurious ever built. It was a car for the newly adventurous among film stars, royalty, and blue-blooded aristocracy, owner-drivers prepared to ditch the chauffeur and the Rolls-Royce Phantom VI limousine which the Camargue replaced at the top of the family tree.

In its day, the Rolls-Royce Camargue was the most expensive production car in the world – but its production standards were so high that during eleven years, only 530 (535 including prototypes and a single, specially commissioned, Bentley Camargue) were made. It was a car from which to rule the world.

FIRST MANUFACTURED:
1975 (until 1986)
ENGINE:
6,750 cc V8
PERFORMANCE:
Top speed of 120 mph (193 km/h);
0-60 mph (97 km/h) in 11.3 secs
YOU SHOULD KNOW:
Not everyone liked the Camargue's angular, chiselled, Italian sleekness, or even the exotic dashboard styled by Sergio Pininfarina to suggest an aircraft cockpit. But the attention to comfort included super-wide doors to allow easy access to the rear seats and a second door handle inside, placed so that a passenger didn't have the bother of leaning forward to open it to get out again.

Rover P6B 3500S

In the mid 1960s, when Rover discovered that Buick had developed a compact V8 which proved unsuitable for their own, US Interstate-cruising sized saloons, they bought it. The small-block, aluminium 3.5 litre engine generated some 50% more power than Rover's existing staple. Proudly, after improving the engine in house, and successfully testing it in their P5 model, the company spelled out its new P6 version as the Three Thousand Five in 1968. By 1970, the year Rover revamped its entire P6 range as the Mark II, or 'B' (officially – but it's often known as the Series II), it was plain 3500; and in 1971, the addition of a four-speed manual version was designated the Rover P6B 3500S.

Everything came together. The P6 had been designed from scratch in 1963. It had de Dion tube suspension at the back, four wheel disc brakes, full synchromesh, and a unitary construction 'inspired' by the Citroen DS. It also had a clutch of industry safety awards. A fortuitous feature was the front suspension, designed among other things to maximize the space in the engine compartment. The Buick V8, when it arrived, squeezed in – but the Mark II upgrades included reshaping the hood to improve the fit and the air intake, and a new radiator grille. Inside, 1971 brought smart piping to the leather trim and a plethora of circular gauges and rotary switches (for Rover at the time, 'old' was linear, and old-style circular was 'new'). The lighter (than the P5B), more powerful and faster P6B 3500S was now top of the Rover range. Police forces loved it.

With a top speed of 124 mph (200 km/h), Rover hoped the car's otherwise adult solidity would entice drivers as an alternative to BMWs and Alfa Romeos. Aside for the unreliable gearbox, it was a worthy ambition.

FIRST MANUFACTURED:
1971 (until 1977)
ENGINE:
3,528 cc V8
PERFORMANCE:
Top speed of 124 mph (200 km/h);
0-60 mph (97 km/h) in 9 secs
YOU SHOULD KNOW:
Often called the P6 NADA ('North American Dollar Area' – an acronym dropped officially in 1967), the left-hand drive Federal 3500S combined Mark I and II features, and was the best of the lot. Alas! Wraparound bumpers, air scoops on the hood, air-conditioning and 'Icelert' sensors on the grille (to warn you of falling outside temperatures) didn't compensate for unreliability.

Plenty of V8 power made this Rover something of a favourite with the British Police.

Rover SD1

The Rover SD1 of 1976 inspired either ecstasy or apoplexy. As a member of the new British Leyland group, Rover now had major in-house competitors like Triumph and Jaguar, with whom it was expected to share parts and develop discrete elements of the company's extended range. It also had a brand-new factory of its own to produce the fruits of its Specialist Division – but that couldn't happen until the Division had learned the lessons of compromise from its early efforts.

The SD1 went into production on a wave of infectious optimism shared by industry critics and the public. It was fast and safe – crash-tested, crumple-zoned, ergonomically brilliant and innovative. With the ever-versatile and seemingly endless tuneability of the 3.5 litre Buick V8 (though perhaps after more than a decade it could be called Rover's own), it made the most of its low weight. People

FIRST MANUFACTURED:
1976 (until 1986)
ENGINE:
3,528 cc V8
PERFORMANCE:
Top speed of 130 mph (208 km/h);
0-60 mph (97 km/h) in 7.7 secs
YOU SHOULD KNOW:
In its lifetime, the SD1 was never marketed by that name. The 14 different versions (including the Vanden Plas and Vitesse of the 1980s) were identified by their engines.

admired its sporty handling, composed ride and modern design. It looked like a Ferrari Daytona (check the front end light assembly) with a hatchback by Pininfarina; and until Rover introduced a range of smaller engines some time later, it had a performance to match. The executive market for which it was intended glowed with reflected glory at its racing and rallying success. Margaret Thatcher's Cabinet ministers all wanted one, and it was photographed underneath Concorde's needle nose as the 1976 Car of the Year.

Unfortunately, the new icon of post-war British car design was a manufacturing crock. Initial reaction had made favourable comparison with Jaguar and its ilk. Instead of upgrading the SD1, its price and build quality to match, Rover tried to give it a more 'economy' feel. Simultaneously, the first batch of cars began to rust, break down, and fall apart. Conceived as a world contender, the SD1's future literally rotted away.

The SD1 was handsome, but a leading contender when it comes to choosing the British production car with the worst-ever build quality.

Beware of the Talbot Sunbeam Lotus – a true wolf in innocent-looking sheep's clothing.

Talbot Sunbeam Lotus

The Talbot Sunbeam Lotus is Hannibal Lecter garbed in the fluffiest of white woolly fleeces. If you're racing against it, rallying or just taking off informally from a contested red light, this car will rip your throat out before parking neatly to offer you Elastoplast therapy. If, on the other hand, you are the driver, you may wear your smirk with vicarious pride for the many who would love to be in your place.

There's a thoroughly professional construct underlying the corporate and political face-offs that surrounded the car's genesis. Chrysler inherited Hillman's Imp and Avenger when it acquired Britain's Rootes Group with a subsequent governmental condition that it maintain the Linwood factory in Scotland. To satisfy many competing demands, including its own to create a serious Group 4 racing contender, Chrysler (by now Chrysler UK and Europe), developed the agreed new supermini, the Sunbeam, from existing Imp and Avenger parts, as a fairly conventional three-door hatchback. The Sunbeam's shortened Avenger wheelbase was, of course, a highly exploitable rear wheel drive. Lotus, invited to the party after the 1977 launch, installed their own 2.2 litre twin-cam engine and managed to create one of the fastest rallying-potential cars of the era.

Lotus did much more, modifying the suspension and brakes to make the live axle more effective, and insisting on a five-speed ZF gearbox (with first gear canted over to the left in true racing style!). Visually, apart from sills above the wheel arches, there wasn't much to reveal its lightning secrets; and the Chrysler Sunbeam Lotus was presented at the Geneva Motor Show of 1979. By then, Chrysler had sold itself to Peugeot, and the road-going version was delivered as the Talbot Sunbeam Lotus.

Never mind the politics. It won the 1980 Lombard RAC Rally and the 1981 World Rally Championship. Its apparent innocence makes you shiver. It's magnificent.

FIRST MANUFACTURED:
1979 (until 1981)
ENGINE:
2,174 cc Slant Four
PERFORMANCE:
Top speed of 121 mph (195 km/h);
0-60 mph (97 km/h) in 7.4 secs
YOU SHOULD KNOW:
Very seldom has a race or rally car been conceived, designed, tested, homologated and raced (with success) as quickly as the Talbot Sunbeam Lotus. Ultra-professionalism extended to works drivers including Henri Toivonen, Guy Frequelin, Tony Pond and even Stig Blomqvist.

Triumph Stag

The Triumph Stag was launched as British Leyland's four-seat, fully convertible, sporting grand tourer challenge to the Mercedes-Benz 280SL. It was the culmination of Italian designer Giovanni Michelotti's long collaboration with Triumph, who insisted that Michelotti's wholly original ideas should not be compromised by the 1968 merger of BMC and Leyland-Rover-Triumph. Like the hero of a Greek tragedy, the Stag came into being bearing the seeds of its own destruction.

British Leyland took over shortly after the Stag's development was up and running. Already, the car was seen to be creating a niche overlooked by its competitors: a posh, 'gentleman's tourer' (later pinpointed, amusingly, as 'a sort of British Thunderbird'), powered by its own, British, V8 engine. Rover already had a masterly 3.5 litre V8 – but Rover were Triumph's arch-rivals, and their parents' shotgun marriage was not to permit them to wrestle Triumph's baby away. The Stag's bespoke engine block went ahead. In essence, two Triumph 1.5 litre Slant Four engines were joined on a common crankshaft to create the Stag's double overhead camshaft 3 litre V8. With the water pump mounted too high in the 'V' of the cylinder heads, the coolant level quickly dropped. Blown gaskets and overheating wrecked dozens of engines.

When it worked, the Stag was a refined cruiser with great handling and impeccable style, but long before its launch it had been subverted by Leyland bean-counters. They demanded cheap versions of every component and fabric. Allied to poor build and laughable quality control, British Leyland's every action devalued Michelotti's fabulous concept. Some problems were resolved in the 1973 Mark 2, but it was too late to affect public confidence.

The Triumph Stag's demise broke hearts, but history holds it dear (*Classic & Sports Car* magazine noted it was 'the most stolen classic car'). And so it should.

FIRST MANUFACTURED:
1970 (until 1977)
ENGINE:
2,998 cc DOHC V8
PERFORMANCE:
Top speed of 118 mph (190 km/h);
0-60 mph (97 km/h) in 9.3 secs
YOU SHOULD KNOW:
The Triumph Stag made *Time* magazine's 'All-Time Worst Cars' list, characterized as 'a despicable, rotten-to-the-core mockery of a car', though 'lively and fun to drive, as long as it ran'. *Time* also judged that the effect of the chrome-framed windows was 'to put the driver in a shiny aquarium'.

The Stag was a great favourite with sporty drivers and is still loved by classic car fans.

Triumph Dolomite Sprint

FIRST MANUFACTURED:
1973 (until 1980)
ENGINE:
1,998 cc Straight Four
PERFORMANCE:
Top speed 118 mph (190 km/h);
0-60 mph (97 km/h) in 8.4 secs
YOU SHOULD KNOW:
In 1975, the British specialist car maker Panther created a 'mini Rolls-Royce' version of the Triumph Dolomite Sprint. The Panther Rio has hand-beaten panelwork and flaunts an interior of sybaritic leather and walnut luxury – at not much more than three times the price.

The affectionate nickname 'Dolly Sprint' is a measure of the respect aficionados have for the car. Triumph's Dolomite Sprint was a very fast, very clever creation. Its Jekyll was a four-door, traditionally manicured, upmarket saloon calculated to reassure corporate managers of their status, and to persuade them by association of its genteel suitability as an executive-level company fleet vehicle for their colleagues. Its Hyde was invisible engineering that gave the Sprint blistering acceleration and the high-speed stamina to win the British Saloon Car Championships (in 1975 and 1978).

The Sprint was the 2 litre performance version of the Triumph Dolomite luxury saloon – but the Sprint's engine was technically much more original than the usual upgrade. Len Dawtrey, one of Spen King's dedicated design team, found a way to actuate 16 valves off a single camshaft. His method sited the plugs centrally in the cylinder head, the ideal position to create real gains in horsepower from the available engine. Now it sounds simple. Then, it was revolutionary, and the cylinder head won a British Design Council award in 1974. Everything else had to be improved to tame the dramatic increase in power. In overdrive, Sprint Jekyll cruised with smooth refinement; but when push needed a shove, Sprint Hyde responded with brusque urgency and violence that really did seem to belong to a different character. Otherwise sharp handling was prone to understeer on tight corners – but drivers got used to it, and enjoyed the Sprint's dual nature.

A walnut fascia, thick carpeting, armchair comfort and every conceivable facility added to the pleasure (and distractions) of driving a car which demanded focus and concentration; but the real enemy was British Leyland's pennypinching and slapdash quality control, which brutalized the Sprint's reputation. Happily, surviving Sprints are still terrorizing the world of motor sports.

The Dolomite was great fun to drive, with a luxurious interior.

TVR 3000S

Since 1947, every TVR sports car has been the love child of one of the company's various owners, all of whom have devoted themselves to their passion with a usually reckless regard for its cost in any form. It's magnificent – it always has been – but it's not car manufacturing. The TVR 3000S exemplifies the company's totally individualistic approach to design; and it is a landmark, the ultimate expression of that approach, pointing both backwards at TVR's history of achievement, and forwards to the way ahead. Almost literally.

The TVR 3000S only happened because the company's then-current owner wanted a convertible. Since every TVR is hand-made, his car wasn't just a decapitated 3000M coupe, though it shared everything mechanical. The windscreen was dropped. Every body panel to the rear of the hood had to be re-cut to lower the doors for a racier feel, and to fulfil the redesigned rear section to include (for the first time) proper boot-space. The side windows could be removed, but not rolled down, and the hood was a vintage-style foldaway. The dashboard had to be re-organized round the transmission tunnel: which made the speedometer on right-hand drive models invisible to the driver, and hid the rev counter on left-hand drives. Lower, sleeker, and (with the 'M' hood unchanged) meaner by far than the coupe or its hatchback Taimar version, the production TVR 3000S incorporated the company's past and future. It is mystifying that no-one had previously tried it.

They certainly loved it. Its performance was already proven, and it got better. Turbo versions achieved 145 mph (233 km/h). TVR's California agent was terrified by crowds brandishing wads of dollar bills in the hope of securing one, but TVR could only make 258 in two years. Its vicissitudes continued - but the first production convertible saw TVR through the 'coma years', and secured its future.

The 3000S was a joy to drive for anyone who was lucky enough to get hold of one.

FIRST MANUFACTURED:
1978 (until 1979)
ENGINE:
2,994 cc V6
PERFORMANCE:
Top speed of 133 mph (214 km/h);
0-60 mph (97 km/h) in 7.5 secs
YOU SHOULD KNOW:
Finding replacement parts for the TVR 3000S (or any of the TVR M series) is a matter of 'automotive archaeology', because the company was completely dependent on raiding the parts boxes of other manufacturers in the first place. Whether it's a door latch, windscreen, or even engine part, identical models often have different, frequently untraceable, components.

Car jargon can be confusing. Below are some of the more common abbreviations and terms.

Some Common Abbreviations:

ABS	antilock braking system
ATV	all terrain vehicle
AWD/4WD	all-wheel drive (four-wheel drive)
DOHC	See OHC
ESC	electronic stability control
EXT	extended cab (four doors on a pickup truck)
FMR	front mid-engine rear wheel drive
FWD	front-wheel drive
GRP	glass-reinforced plastic
GT	gran turismo (grand tourer: high-performance luxury auto for long-distance driving)
GTi	gran turismo-injection (grand tourer with fuel injection engine)
GTO	gran turismo omologato (GT car homologated for racing)
LWB	long wheelbase
MPV	multi-purpose vehicle
NASCAR	National Association for Stock Car Auto Racing
OHC	overhead cam (DOHC = dual OHC or twin cam; SOHC = single OHC)
OHV	overhead valve
PZEV	partial zero-emissions vehicle
RMR	rear mid-engine rear-wheel drive
RS	Rally Sport
RWD	rear-wheel drive
SAV	sports activity vehicle (alternative to SUV, see below)
SOHC	See OHC
SUV	sports utility vehicle (minivan/truck, usually AWD for on-and off-road driving)
SWB	short wheelbase

Note on Horsepower

The power that an engine produces is measured in units of horsepower (or 'horses'). Some power is used up by the drivetrain so the actual horsepower available for propulsion is less than the gross power that the engine produces. This net power is known as **brake horsepower (bhp)** although it is often referred to simply as horsepower or hp.

In Europe and Japan, power is measured in **P**ferde**S**tärke ('horse strength' in German) which is also known as metric horsepower or DIN 1 PS/DIN = 0.986 hp. So PS/DIN and bhp are nearly equivalent to each other, but not quite.

Note on Engine Displacement (Capacity)

In Europe and Japan, manufacturers normally give displacement data in cubic centimetres (cc). In the USA, it is conventionally given in litres or cubic inches. Throughout this book the data is given in cc except for cars manufactured in the USA for which it is given in litres (l) with the equivalent cubic inch displacement (cid) in brackets. 1 cu in =16.387 cc.

Car Terms:

cabriolet	car with a removable/retractable soft top; convertible; drophead coupe
coupe	two-door car with hard top
crossover	vehicle built on a car platform with characteristics of van or SUV
drivetrain	See powertrain
drophead	See cabriolet
doors:	
butterfly	slide upwards and move outwards (similar to scissor)
gullwing	hinged at the top to lift upwards
scissor	slide upwards from single fixed hinge at end of windscreen
suicide	hinged at the rear rather than the front (also known as coach doors)
estate car	station wagon; shooting brake
flathead	See sidevalve
hardtop	a car design that has no central roof struts (B-pillars)
homologated	certified (or approved) as meeting the standard requirements for a particular class of car when taking part in racing
inline	See straight
monocoque	a way of manufacturing a car as an integrated piece (unibody) instead of a body mounted onto a separately built chassis
muscle car	large, fast gas-guzzler with supercharged V8 engine
pickup	truck-like vehicle (either two- or four-door) with open load bed at back
pillars	the struts that hold up the car roof.
A-pillars	struts at either side of front windscreen
B-pillars	centre struts behind the front doors
C-pillars	struts at either side of rear window
pony car	compact performance car of the late 1950s to 1970, inspired by Ford Mustang design
pushrod	an engine with an overhead valve (OHV) design
powertrain	parts of the car that deliver power to the road – engine, transmission, differential, driveshafts, drive wheels; drivetrain
roadster	two-seater convertible sports car
running gear	1. suspension, shock absorbers and steering *or* 2. transmission, driveshaft and wheels
saloon	four-door (family) hardtop car; sedan
sedan	See saloon
sidevalve	engine design in which valves are positioned at the side of the combustion chamber instead of at the cylinderhead – hence also known as 'flathead'
straight *or* inline	arrangement of cylinders in an engine. Cylinders are either in a line or a V (with variations such as staggered or W)
supercar	car with high horsepower engine for high speed and fast acceleration
woodie	estate car with a wooden body
ute	Australian utility vehicle See pickup

Alamy /Paul Broadbent 5 picture 5, 9 bottom right, 20, 86; /Buzz Pictures 96 bottom left, 100-101; /Dale Drinnon 28-29; /Andy Drisdale 107; /Chuck Eckert 7 picture 5, 24 left, 35; /Alex Friedel 36-37; /Heritage Image Partnership 14-15; /ImageBroker 91; Andy Johnson 118-119; /Simon Margetson Travel 59; /John Marian/ Transtock Inc. 16, 9 left, 46-47; /Bob Masters Classic Car Images 22-23; /Motoring Picture Library 50-51, 88-89, 152-153; /Phil Talbot 5 picture 1, 32-33, 68-69, 114-115, 154; /Jonathan Tennant 58; /Harald Woeste 41

Ron Callow 88 bottom left, 88 bottom right, 89 bottom left, 89 bottom right

Corbis/Car Culture 138-139

LAT Photographic 2 bottom left, 2 bottom right, 2-3 bottom centre, 3 bottom right, 3 bottom left, 5 picture 2, 5 picture 3, 5 picture 4, 5 picture 6, 5 picture 7, 6 picture 3, 6 picture 4, 6 picture 5, 6 picture 7, 7 picture 1, 7 picture 2, 7 picture 4, 7 picture 6, 8-9 main, 8 bottom left, 8 bottom right, 12, 13, 14-15, 21, 24-25 main, 25 bottom left, 25 bottom right, 26, 27, 30, 34, 38, 39, 40 42-43 45, 49, 53, 56-57 main, 56 bottom left, 57 bottom left, 60-61, 64-65, 67, 70, 76-77, 78, 80-81, 87, 90, 92-93, 94, 96-97 main, 98, 99, 102, 108-109, 111, 113, 116, 117, 120-121, 122, 123, 124, 128-129, 131, 134-135, 136, 137, 141, 144-145, 146 bottom right, 147 bottom left, 148-149, 150, 155, 160, 161, 162-163, 166, 171, 172, 173

National Motor Museum 7 picture 3, 7 picture 7, 10-11, 17, 18-19, 31, 44, 48, 57 bottom right, 62, 72-73, 74, 79, 83, 96 bottom right, 97 bottom left, 97 bottom right, 103, 104-105, 106, 110, 112, 126, 127, 130, 140, 142-143, 146-147 main, 146 bottom left, 151, 158-159, 164, 165; /Nick Georgano 6 picture 1, 24 bottom right, 52, 147 bottom right, 170; /Nicky Wright 6 picture 2, 13, 63, 66, 82

PA Photos/Barratts/S&G Barratts/EMPICS Archive 71

Rex Features/Magic Car Pictures 54-55, 84-85, 132-133, 138-139, 168-169; /National Motor Museum 156-157, 167

Shutterstock/Magicinfoto 75

Thinkstock/suricoma cover

Wikipedia/Arpingstone 56 bottom right, 95

Some of the material in this book first appeared in
501 Must-Drive Cars.